CW00551048

Rachel Mann is a priest, poe[...]
She has written fifteen books
shortlisted for the Michael [...]
on BBC radio and is a regular contributor to 'Thought for the Day'. She is Visiting Teaching Fellow in Creative Writing at the Manchester Writing School and, currently, she is Archdeacon of Salford and Bolton, in the Diocese of Manchester.

DO NOT BE AFRAID

The joy of waiting in a time of fear

Rachel Mann

First published in Great Britain in 2024

SPCK
SPCK Group
Studio 101
The Record Hall
16–16A Baldwin's Gardens
London EC1N 7RJ
www.spckpublishing.co.uk

British Library Cataloguing-in-Publication Data
A catalogue record for this book is available from the British Library

ISBN 978–0–281–09001–3
eBook ISBN 978–0–281–09002–0

1 3 5 7 9 10 8 6 4 2

Typeset by Fakenham Prepress Solutions, Fakenham, Norfolk NR21 8NL
First printed in Great Britain by Clays Ltd, Bungay, Suffolk

eBook by Fakenham Prepress Solutions, Fakenham, Norfolk NR21 8NL

Produced on paper from sustainable sources

Contents

Contents

THE THIRD WEEK OF ADVENT

THE FOURTH WEEK OF ADVENT

Foreword

Unexpected, unwanted, unremitting and seemingly endless waiting can be horrible. Years ago, I remember getting muddled over the time of a flight and arriving at the airport ridiculously early. Cursing my mistake, I realised I had about seven hours to kill. What would I do? How many flat whites can any man drink? How many tours of the duty-free emporium can anyone endure? And even peering through the window of the high-end Burberry, Louis Vuitton and Rolex boutiques can exhaust only so many minutes.

Then it dawned on me: a wisdom I have been very slow to learn. That this moment now is all I have; and, if I was to find meaning or joy in any of life's many moments, it had to be found in this unexpected and unwanted waiting.

This wasn't time to kill, but time to ravish; the only time I would ever have. More than this: somehow in the waiting, however lonely and however frustrating, there is also the anticipation of the greater joys that are around the corner.

'I wait for the LORD,' says the psalmist. 'My soul waits, and in his word I hope; my soul waits for the Lord, more than those who watch for the morning.' These words from Psalm 130 capture a deep truth: that human beings have always known the cost and the hope and, ultimately, the joy that is found in waiting.

In this luminous and insightful book, Rachel Mann taps into this ancient wisdom and recasts it for our present impatient age, obsessed as it is with the instant gratification offered by social media, as well as our seeming addiction to speed of action and thought. She reminds us that, in a world where many use their financial and social capital to avoid – as much as possible! – the boredoms and frustrations generated by waiting, there is glory to be found in waiting for the Lord and seeking hope in the good news of Jesus Christ. And what better time to attend to this good news than during this great season of watching and waiting, Advent?

At the same time, Rachel doesn't shy away from just how annoying our everyday experiences of waiting can be. She talks with humour, candour and insight about everything from waiting for a hospital appointment to being stuck in a traffic jam to the indignities that can come with being disabled in a society not quite as understanding as we might hope it to be. She knows only too well that waiting is rarely fun, and she is determined not to be pious about its irritations. Indeed, one of the many things that is impressive about *Do Not Be Afraid* is Rachel's willingness to be vulnerable and real about the cost not only of living in a fallen and imperfect world, but of following Jesus in it. She reminds me that being honest with God and one another is important in addressing the ups and downs of life.

Waiting – and the joy that awaits us – is central to the Advent season, as I said above. Moreover, we see the frightening horrors that are engulfing and constraining our world at the moment – war, climate crisis and rank injustice – and are reminded of those other Advent themes that speak of final things.

Waiting *for* the Lord and waiting *on* the Lord are part of the holy gift of this season of Advent. We are waiting for a better way. We are watching for justice to come. And as we wait, whether for the return of Jesus in glory or for the breaking forth of Christmas joy, we are obedient to our vocation to love God and neighbour with everything we have.

Throughout the book, Rachel uses her wonderful gifts as a poet, priest and theologian to turn our attention to different modes of waiting, but always keeps the focus on Jesus. He is the one we wait for. He is the one who is waiting for us. She reminds us that those famous words of Isaiah, 'Do not be afraid …', are not just a quotable piece of wisdom to adorn a social media post; they are an abiding call from God to trust ever more deeply in him, perhaps most especially when the world seems closest to falling apart. In this book, Rachel returns again and again to the awesome trustworthiness of Jesus who, as God-with-us, knows the cost of being human from the inside, but equally brings us back home to the Father in love and forgiveness.

I trust that, like me, you will find that this Advent pilgrimage stirs your imagination and stokes in your heart the love for God's redeeming work. I pray that *Do Not Be Afraid* helps you not only to discover the gracious presence of Jesus in your call to watch and wait for him, but also prepares you to greet him once again with joy on Christmas Day.

Stephen Cottrell
Archbishop of York

Introduction

It happens everywhere: at home and at bus stops, at airports and on the tube … in shops and at the gym. It happens in hospitals and in our cars. It happens when we pick up our phones and laptops. It happens when we queue up to get into football matches, cricket games, and to see our favourite musical artists. It happens to all of us. Whether we are rich or poor, and whatever our cultural background and position in society, it cannot be avoided. More often than not, it is experienced as annoying and, at times, as infuriating. Waiting is everywhere.

This book explores the frustrations, irritations and inconveniences we associate with waiting. It is also an invitation to sense the richness and promise of God in the midst of these everyday experiences. Stuck on your phone in a queue for customer service? Hanging around for ages to be seen by a doctor at A&E? Even – in a different way – waiting, waiting, waiting for the world to change for the better? For all the discomfort and, indeed, sheer anger and disappointment that waiting can conjure, I think the grace and gift of God can not only be found in waiting but is often discovered most profoundly there. *Do Not Be Afraid* dwells deeply on the very many modes of waiting and says that, in their midst, there can be an encounter with something greater and holier.

Waiting can be full of joy. Why? Because it is part of the story and glory of God. Some of the wonder of Advent lies in God's invitation to wait on and with and for the one who is our salvation, Jesus Christ. Jesus comes into our midst and shows us the deepest reality of the world. He shows us that, for all of life's irritations, frustrations and – frankly – sheer grimness, the universe is made in love and we are called to joyous celebration. We need to hear this. Well, I do anyway. I cannot be alone in needing – sometimes quite desperately! – the reality of God's joy. We live in a time when fear and anxiety threaten to overwhelm us. The after-effects of the pandemic have left many exhausted. I also know a lot of people, perhaps especially those who are younger, who feel genuine fear for the future, a fear stoked by the realities of the climate crisis and the growing lack of trust in democratic institutions. For very many, even to think about the implications for the coming years is to encounter fear. Those who long for change and justice in a world on fire and in a Church in meltdown can be left feeling as if the very idea of waiting is not only exhausting and irritating, but deeply offensive.

However, waiting can also be charged with expectation. Waiting is one of the richest spiritual seams in the Bible and in Christian tradition and it is always tied to hope. The psalmist says, 'I waited patiently for the LORD; he inclined to me and heard my cry.'[1] The people of God, cry out 'How long, O LORD?', yearning and waiting for salvation.[2] Jesus Christ comes into the world as the one long waited for, and as the servant who waits on others and on whom we are called to wait. At Advent we actively anticipate and pray for Christ's return, as well as wait with hope to meet him again at Christmas. This kind of waiting is creative, inviting us into service as well as stirring up our hunger for justice and love. There can even be a theological power in frustration and boredom – the offering of space to plan, prepare and join in prayerful solidarity with others.

Advent – this great season of discipline, preparation, fasting and, indeed, of waiting – offers us an extraordinary opportunity to attend to the work and love of God; to wait on the one who travels towards Bethlehem to be born and who will return in glory. Thanks be to the living God, that even if there are times where waiting can seem endless – indeed, sometimes the world seems to have the character of C. S. Lewis's Narnia under the rule of the White Witch, where it is winter but Christmas never arrives – ultimately, God cannot be deflected or kept down. Advent offers a holy opportunity to wait on the one who stands in solidarity with us; the one who calls all of us – whether we think we are saved or not, whether we think we are pilgrims on the Way or feel lost and afraid or tempted to despair – into the fullness of life. As Advent begins, let us wait with hope and joy; let us come to a deeper trust in God, which means we do not need to rush (as modern secular Advent wants) to get to Bethlehem and birth with a barely restrained glee. Let us dwell in these coming days of Advent in the gift of waiting on and for and with the Gift.

The First Sunday of Advent
The joy of waiting ... 'Do not fear'

Fear. It's the only word that captures what I felt. We were drifting slowly out, deeper into the Caribbean Sea while the captain of our little canoe tried and tried to get its single outboard motor restarted. Every time it sputtered with promise, it died again. For the first time on that journey, I had to accept that we might need to swim for it ... and that scared the life out of me because I was no swimmer and the shore was at least 100 metres away.

Just twelve hours before, things had been so different. We had travelled up Jamaica's Black River to visit some friends for an afternoon of food and dancing. We were full of excitement and anticipation. The trip – which had taken us from white-sand beaches out onto the sea and then up through the estuary of the river and into mangrove swamps – was a great adventure. Yes, it was slow going in the little boat with its tiny motor, but the six of us felt no fear. It was another beautiful Caribbean day, full of light and warmth and the sounds of the bush. Everything was going to plan.

Almost as soon as we started back home, all that changed. The engine kept cutting out and, as we eked our way back down the river, the bush and jungle were transformed by night. The soundscape became menacing rather than exciting, and the small boat seemed like no shelter at all. Finally, as we 'put-putted' out to sea, the little outboard motor gave up the fight entirely. The boat owner was relaxed – 'No worries,' he said. Was that just to reassure us as he tried and failed to get the engine going? Those of us who were passengers fell silent. I suspect some of us began to pray.

Then, for the first time, to distract myself, I gazed heavenward and stupidly said out loud, 'What's that?' For what I saw was something I'd never encountered before. It was as if icing sugar had been cast across the night sky. It was pale dust glimmering in the dark. It was wonder in white. The person in front of me, looking upwards in response to my words, said, with exhaustion in his voice, 'Oh, it's just the Milky Way.'

That night, over thirty years ago, has never let me go. Yes, I was transfixed with fear, but that's not really the reason it has stayed with me. The truly unforgettable thing was viewing the Milky Way in all its awesome intensity for the first time in my life. Though my friend called it 'just' the Milky Way, for me it was a revelation. I looked up and my eyes were met by something that it is only possible to see when there is no light pollution to get in the way: the vast wonder of the galaxy. That night, I witnessed the joy that can be found in the firmament. In a place beyond the shore of safety, I glimpsed aspects of creation usually hidden from me, and received such reassurance.

For me, this story is not only about the casting out of fear. It is also about finding treasure in the waiting. At the heart of what was a genuinely scary experience, I encountered what can only be called 'joy'. I had an overwhelming experience of wonder and delight. For this to happen, I had to be in a place where I was forced to wait on God: where, despite my anxiety and understandable desire to get back to safety as quickly as possible, I had to stop. At the very point when I was not in control, dependent on the canoe captain and the tides and God, I was exactly where I could be surprised by the gift of creation. I looked up and beheld the glory of God and was not afraid.

Fear is a rational reaction to many situations, but at a deep level, as the Bible reminds us, we do not need to be afraid. Isaiah 43:1–3 says that God calls each of us by name and we are his. At the start of this Advent journey of faith and hope, let's remind ourselves of the unconditional generosity and abundance of God's love. No matter what we may face in life, however unequipped we might feel to deal with its challenges, our God is a giver who promises to be with us. That was certainly my experience that night on the Caribbean Sea all those years ago. Thankfully, our captain eventually got the outboard motor running again and saw us home. Before that, however, as we waited on the sea, I received a vision of grace, and I shall be for ever thankful.

Prayer

O Come, O Come Emmanuel,
set us free to wait in longing, hope and trust;
come into our midst once again,
and liberate us to serve in Love. Amen.

Questions

- In what situations and on what occasions have you found God offering you reassurance in the midst of your fear?

- Can you think of a time when taking a risk has led you to encounter more of God's grace?
- In what kind of situations have you been surprised by joy?

Monday
Waiting for insight: Connected

We are all shaped and formed by others. We are influenced and affected by the love or, sadly, the hate, the kindness or the harshness of other people. We all live in the wake and after-flow of other lives. In that sense, these formative experiences may seem to have an inevitable link to cause and effect: I suspect we have all come across the cliché that violence breeds violence. Thus, a person is treated brutally as a child, and – according to popular thinking – they grow up to become a brutal person.

I don't believe in such a mechanistic understanding of human behaviour. My dad experienced a pretty harsh upbringing, but that actually led him to be gentler and kinder. He had witnessed his father, a Great War veteran with an alcohol problem, become violent when he had had too much to drink. Dad couldn't bear seeing his mother take the brunt of her husband's trauma and rage. In the end he stood up to his father, but also decided – in his own parenthood – not to be like him. My dad could be a bluff, firm man, with a pretty tough code, but he was not violent. He didn't want to follow his dad's pattern and he didn't.

Our 'formation' by others can take a quite literal shape, of course. Surely this applies to how we are made in our mother's womb. It is worth dwelling for a moment on this reminder that all of us are shaped and grown as part of another person's body; that from the very outset, we are in the company of another, our mother. Psalm 139 also reminds us that God knows us from before we are born; we are written in the book of love and grace while still in the womb. At birth, we do not become completely separate and discrete beings; we are still made for relationship and dependent on those who care for us for survival and nourishment:

> We learn the world, the first world
> Of love and drool and sweet milk
> Through lips.

> What surprise that prayer shares
> A language with kisses?[1]

Even Our Lord himself undergoes this shaping. He does not arrive out of heaven fully formed. Rather, God empties himself into one such as us, one who knows dependence and vulnerability. Jesus is held and cherished by his mum and dad; he is dandled on their knees. He is fed at the breast and learns a language of love and prayer. The one who grows up to proclaim the Beatitudes was formed in the company of the one who sings the Magnificat; at her breast and in her words and wisdom the Son of God learns to speak of justice, mercy and the purposes of God. Jesus carries Mary throughout his ministry. Part of the power of the tradition of the Pietà, which depicts Mary cradling Jesus' mortal body after his descent from the cross, is how it shows Mary's devotion to the end: she carried him in her womb; she carried him in her heart for his whole life, and at the end, in death, she will not let him fall without loving arms to hold him.

There are other ways in which we may carry others. I carry my dear friend Fr Alan with me every time I preside at the Eucharist. Alan was not my training incumbent, but he was the person from whom I learned to dwell in eucharistic ministry. His style of celebrating the Eucharist was reverential, yet relaxed; theatrical, yet controlled. When he taught me how to preside, I was mesmerised by the dancing choreography of his arms, held in tension with his stillness and his centredness. Nearly twenty years on from the training I received from Alan, the gestures I use and the sense of theatre I bring to the Eucharist reflect what I learned from him. Alan died in 2019, but he is with me every time I say Mass. You can see him in and through me. It's taken me ages to realise this; I have waited half a decade for insight to emerge. Perhaps only in the light of Alan's death have I appreciated it.

Like many foolish people, I've spent large parts of my life wanting to act as if I am myself alone. I've sought to gain distance from those people and those situations which formed me and strike out on my own. I'm not hugely proud of this. But then, so many of us wish to avoid turning into our mother or our father! What I've learned is that we can try to be too individualistic, and that there is nothing to fear from being influenced by others or embracing the goodness of being moulded by the deep ebb and flow of abiding love which quietly forms us.

The Mary who carries Jesus is one who knows what waiting looks like. Until Gabriel appeared, we might say

7

she was waiting for her life to begin (though I would not want to suggest that her life found meaning simply as a 'mother'). It was in carrying God's son that she understood she had always carried within her God's longing for justice and goodness and a world made new; she became the carrier of God's promises. Through Mary, the longings of the whole people of God came alive and she was able to articulate their waiting for good news in the Magnificat.

The promises of God are not found in our separation from others, but in how we dwell in others and they in us. Both the dead and the living whisper in our ears and, we pray, they whisper good and encouraging things. Ultimately, all that we have comes from God; it is all gift and the gift finds its leaven and fullest reality in relationship. In the waiting lies the promise, even – perhaps most especially – when we do not realise we have been waiting. The challenge is to remember this abiding reality and truth at all times: in our relationship with God and with our friends, our families, and in our church and work communities.

Prayer

God who in the tenderness of your love,
always carries us, help us to carry you
and those whom you call us
to serve, this day and always. Amen.

Questions

- To what extent do you think living in an individualistic era is in conflict with being a person of faith?

- How can coming to an appreciation that we 'carry' other people within us help us accept that we are dependent on others and God for our flourishing?
- Think back to a time when you have waited for insight. How was God involved in bringing you to the point of illumination?

Tuesday
Waiting in isolation with others

I'd been dreading the arrival of this day all week. I'd caught it creeping up on me out of the corner of my mind's eye. Now it has arrived, and having had a bad night's sleep, all I want is for it to be over. There is no prospect of that. I have been at the hospital since 8 a.m., though my appointment wasn't officially till 10. I was told to get here early for the prep. Ughh, the prep. Just the word gives me the heebie-jeebies. It wouldn't be so bad, but this is a return visit to the Endoscopy Unit after a failed attempt a few weeks before at what is ordinarily a routine procedure. Though what is 'routine' for the medical staff (and indeed for most patients) is not quite so routine for me. I've got so much historic damage to my remaining bowel that the prospect of a camera investigation – and the associated prospect of agony and bleeding – is disturbing. Indeed, the previous attempt didn't work out. Just trying to get me prepped for the procedure damaged my insides and was excruciating. Today, we're going to have another go, hopefully with a slightly more careful approach (and a lot more sedation).

It is now heading towards 12 noon. My stomach rumbles. My mouth is dry, and not just with stress. I'm not supposed to drink or eat before the procedure. When I'm not rushing to the toilet, I lie down on a trolley in my little cubicle. I have already finished my book and the signal for my phone is terrible. I can't even doom-scroll through my social media feeds. I lie on my cot and listen as the world of the ward unfolds beyond the curtain which separates me from other people and my fate. As I lie there, I want the medical staff to come and take me to the procedure room. At the same time, I don't really want them to take me there at all.

I want the waiting to be over, but what am I waiting for? In one sense, nothing more than a routine medical procedure and test, and for that test to be done with. I want to know the results, good or bad. I wait for the work to begin so that I can just get out of here and on with my day. There is a deeper dimension: I am here with others. As I catch snatches of conversation from beyond my cubicle – 'Do you want sedation?', 'Do you have any allergies?', Sharp scratch', 'I'm scared' – I feel solidarity with my fellow patients. I feel for the patience of the nurses. I sense their tiredness.

It is interesting that such is the nature of the medical unit and such is the intimate and embarrassing – for most – nature of what the medics do here, that this is not a place to talk and share stories. We wait in our cots and cubicles and then we get out of here as soon as we can. Even if we wanted to, we're all too dazed after the procedure to speak. I wait also, in a sense, with the medical teams. They are kind and tender and, in the midst of clinical imperatives, don't forget our humanity. However, they also just want to get us through our test and then on with the next task. The place is so busy and they are so stretched. I've never known this unit so stretched. But here we are, all of us – the patients, the medical staff – waiting with one another. We wait and watch for signs of movement – are they coming for me? Is the treatment room free? – and live, therefore, in an odd kind of tension.

I think we wait with God too – the God who longs to set us free, but who is with us in the midst of our everyday experiences of ordinariness, frustration and fear. The God revealed to us in Jesus Christ has never been afraid of the places where painful, terrible and – well – less than pleasant things happen. There is a reason that we worship a God who goes to the cross. Our God is one who shows solidarity and faithfulness with his people when they face the trials of the wilderness, as when Moses leads them towards the promised land; who goes with his people into exile in Babylon. Our God knows us from the inside out, is caught up in our lives and loves us, despite the fact that we sometimes turn away from him.

I am so conscious that when we find ourselves in situations like those we can face in a hospital we can feel atomised and separated from one another; the sheer stress and distress of facing treatment or surgery or a procedure can push us in on ourselves. While the psalmist might say, 'I waited patiently for the LORD; he inclined to me and heard my cry',[2] in such isolating places it can be difficult for us to wait uncomplainingly and with dignity. We become tired and irritable because we are deprived of food and drink and comforts. Yet, God is there. Not as a kind of cheery, ever-smiling presence urging us to be better and kinder, but in our uneasiness and distress. As I wait, you wait, we wait, God waits. God waits with us, sometimes in our longing just to get through this day ... this situation ... this moment. God, even when we cannot sense him, is present with us on the seemingly endless, lonely road. Bidden or unbidden, God comes.

Prayer

Jesus, when we face times of trial,
grant us the grace to dwell in your love;
as you stand by us, help us to stand by you
in your hour of need. Amen.

Questions

- If it is okay to do so, consider situations where you've felt cut off from others and/or you've just 'had to get through it'. What strategies did you use to help?
- What is the role of prayer in helping us deal with challenging situations?
- 'Bidden or unbidden, God comes.' To what extent do you think that's true?

Wednesday
Waiting to slow down

I am part of a very competitive family. This is manifested especially in how we play games with one another. Whatever we do – board games, card games, even vying to answer first while watching *University Challenge* – we do it to win. The competition is part of the fun. We push each other hard and some of us are reasonably high achievers. Sometimes, when we are together I feel as if we live a kind of 'red-buzzer' life: we want to get to the 'answer' before anyone else and win the point. The red buzzer always beckons. We long to beat the other and fear the ignominy of finding we've buzzed too soon, not knowing the correct answer; nonetheless, sometimes it can feel too risky to wait till the whole question has been posed. Best to dive in … best to press the buzzer first.

I suspect this way of describing family life doesn't sound terribly flattering. It makes us appear as if our only concern is to win at all costs. As it happens, while I think we could turn pretty much anything into a race or competition, my family demonstrates a high level of care and trust. There is a sense of fun behind the race. On one occasion, I remember my younger brother, two of my nephews and I played a silly game with his wife and eldest son, both of whom treat walking anywhere as an Olympic sport. The game: see how far we'd fall behind them as we walked to the tram. In the time it took the sporty couple to reach the tram stop (500 metres away), we'd got 300 metres. Having been oblivious to our dawdling, they were not pleased that we'd slowed up the journey.

Most of the time, I am tempted to race ahead and then wait for others to catch up. I want to go at life at pace. I want to get stuff done quickly. I am not good at keeping in step with the slowest. I do not readily go at the pace of what the theologian Kosuke Koyama calls the 'three mile an hour God'.[3] I want to zoom on to the point of the action. I want to get to the red-buzzer moment. At this time of year, I want to get to the nativity of Christ. I do not really want to dwell on the painfully slow and awkward journey of a heavily pregnant Mary and her husband Joseph as they make their way down to Bethlehem. I do not want to attend to the discomfort of that journey. We will all have sung the classic children's carol, 'Little Donkey'. It may not be a biblical story, but for all the sweetness of the song, the idea of travelling to Bethlehem from Nazareth using a donkey is not hugely romantic or appealing. Donkeys – tough and resilient, but slow, slow, slow. I do not want to attend to the sheer time such a journey would have taken and, crucially, the anxieties and fears that would likely have emerged as the Holy Family undertook it. 'Will we even get there?' 'Where is God in all this?'

The journey of the Holy Family reminds us that though the pace is often slow and painstaking, it is also magnificent. For their journey is pregnant with wonder and promise and surely grants space to reflect and ponder. I imagine that Mary and Joseph – both together and individually

– would have been full of anticipation and hope for what was to come. I like to imagine that as they travelled they began to see that waiting on the birth of God in Jesus was a space for thanksgiving and prayer. Even if Mary wanted, near the end, simply to give birth, this time of travelling granted room for her heart to grow with expectation and love.

Recently, my mum visited me for a holiday. She cannot walk very far or very fast, but she does want to go places and try. It would, I guess, be convenient for us, her children, if she decided to allow us to push her in a wheelchair. She prefers to walk. It is her way. Though she will never hit the pace I need to meet my exercise targets, I respect her desire to be independent. Nonetheless, when Mum came to stay and we headed out on trips to National Trust properties or simply went shopping around town, it was almost impossible to resist my instinct to race ahead heedlessly. Indeed, on at least one occasion I did that. My default reaction was then to wait for her to catch up, because my speed, in my head, is the correct one. It took me several days to learn the pace of my mum and stick with it. It was as if she had been waiting for me to slow down all week.

I realised that getting in step with my mum was not only the right and kind thing to do but entailed getting in harmony with the speed of God. In the Gospels, there is never a sense of Jesus rushing or running. He doesn't dash into Jerusalem in a chariot or even gallop on a horse. His ordinary speed is walking pace, and he travels in step with those who require his love and healing. He journeys slowly enough that others' needs can be heard and heeded. Jesus walks alongside those in the greatest hardship, and he invites us too to get in step with holiness.

Ultimately, the pace of God is the only pace that matters. As we have seen, it is not the pace which rushes or takes the easiest route. It is the pace which is needful for salvation and hope and promise. It is a human pace, and perhaps most of all the pace of the vulnerable, the bewildered, the lost and powerless; of those seeking to find the way. It is the pace of the Holy Family on their way to Bethlehem. It is the pace of those who wait on God before they act. That is the pace I should like to learn, so I can slow down and get in alignment with God. I should like to walk (or travel – if I am ever a wheelchair user) at the speed of the God who waits for me to adopt the pace needed to get to Bethlehem at the needful time. In doing so, I might just spot more of what he is up to in the world.

God waits for us to slow down. I wait to learn such wisdom.

Prayer

Generous God,
you greet our hurry with stillness and calm;
thank you that you wait for us
to find our way back to holiness. Amen.

Questions

- When has slowing down (and perhaps waiting) aided your connection with God or brought insight into a situation?

17

- What have you learned from these experiences about how to conduct your life?
- Jesus does not hurry. How does this challenge you to live differently?

Thursday
Waiting on the word: Luke 1:26–38

In the many encounters between the Divine and human beings in the Bible, a mark of God's authentic and definitive work of love and salvation is his call on normal people's lives. This call transforms ordinary folk into extraordinary servants of God. They become, in their sundry ways, those who wait on the living God. God calls to Abram and Sarai, to Moses, to Elijah and Elisha, to the prophets Isaiah and Jeremiah, and many others. God calls and his people are invited to respond. Those who respond are lifted up: not as tyrants to lord it over others, but rather as servants who wait on the one who serves all. Perhaps this is never clearer than in the annunciation, the Blessed Virgin Mary's encounter with the angel Gabriel in Luke's Gospel.

Angel, in Latin, quite literally means 'messenger, envoy or one that announces'. Gabriel, then, is the herald and ambassador of God. God has despatched someone who can represent God himself to others. Indeed, in the Hebrew biblical tradition, Gabriel, as an angel, is yet more: he also represents the very presence of God. Naturally, Gabriel speaks first – 'Greetings, favoured one! The Lord is with you.'[4] Gabriel comes to announce favour and blessing. In an awesome and awe-filled moment, the ambassador and herald of God delivers a message that will change the universe.

Yet, as ever, God surprises us and disrupts our expectations. In our world, at least, an envoy or ambassador 'waits upon' a monarch or president. He or she speaks and relates directly to the 'head of state'. In diplomacy, 'waiting upon' is part of the protocol of power and authority in which all the respect and honour due is shown to one of high position and renown. Yet, the person on whom God's emissary waits is not a king or emperor or princeling, but someone who is little more than a child, and a girl at that. A girl who is the daughter of peasants!

It is perhaps unsurprising that Mary is perplexed and bewildered by Gabriel's grand, ambassadorial greeting, indeed, maybe even suspicious of it. 'Greetings, favoured one! The Lord is with you.' What unexpected words to be said to someone of her status. It is clear that, insofar as Mary is expected to respond to Gabriel's declaration, she is uncertain how to do so. Perhaps she senses risk and danger in God's approach. And, however we interpret what comes next, it appears her instinct is right: for not only is she told that she is favoured by God, but that she is going to have a God-blessed son, the result of being 'overshadowed' by the power of the Holy Spirit. And yet, as she points out, she is a 'virgin' – *parthenos* – or 'maiden'. She may not even have had her first period. What response does Mary make? 'Here am I, the servant of the Lord; let it be with me according to your word.'[5]

Feminist analyses of this encounter are well known. These have ranged from concerns about casting a 'young woman/girl' as a compliant handmaid unable to grant consent, through to questions about whether the text implies that Mary is a victim of rape.[6] Even if one queries the legitimacy of feminist perspectives, there is simply no doubt that, textually, the images created by this encounter are disconcerting. A girl meeting the majesty of God is one thing; a girl being told she will conceive a son via the 'overshadowing' power of the Holy Spirit is another. If this is God's call, then it is certainly intrusive, verging on the abusive: power is massively skewed towards God, and the whole scene gives the impression of a fait accompli.

Yet Luke's account shows that Mary's response is significant; that her willingness to unite her will and purposes to those of God is no mere afterthought. There is a quiet but extraordinary and deeply prophetic determination in her words. I am reminded of the prophet Isaiah when he says, 'Here I am' in Isaiah 6:8. This is one who has earlier exclaimed, 'Woe is me, for I am undone! Because I am a man of unclean lips.' God calls the unlikely and Mary joins a long line of those who will take their place in God's wondrous work of transformation, justice and love. Mary speaks and claims her place. She will not simply be done to but will turn God's invitation into service and action. She will be a voice for the voiceless; she will wait upon the Lord who comes not to be served but to serve.

There is no doubt that Gabriel's encounter with Mary continues to raise questions in the modern era about consent and agency. I do not underestimate these. However, I also find in the first chapter of Luke a young woman seeking dignity in the face of divine majesty. Here is a

21

peasant girl daring to speak to God's ambassador. She has courage and authority. A young girl who has no voice and little agency claims both for herself.

I also think Gabriel, who represents the very presence of the Lord, surprises us with joy. He waits upon a girl without status, position or fame and greets her with all the honour due to a queen. She is a peasant queen who will bear a peasant God, and I hope you can see why, for some, Mary is the Queen of Heaven. As she embraces God's invitation to be the bearer of God, the *theotokos*, she finds her prophetic voice. Indeed, a few months after her encounter with Gabriel, Mary will proclaim her famous Magnificat.[7] These words of justice, comfort and challenge echo down the ages, shaping the community of faith and transforming our world to this day. When Mary sings, 'My soul magnifies the Lord, and my spirit rejoices in God my Saviour, for he has looked with favour on the lowliness of his servant...', she reminds us that no one is beyond the joy of being called to wait on the Lord. Service is the first vocation of the most insignificant or the most exalted.

Prayer

Servant God,
thank you for your faithfulness;
grant us the grace to recognise
you when you come to wait on us.
Help us to be bold in our response. Amen.

Questions

- What difference does it make that God comes to dwell with us as an ordinary human being rather than as a privileged or powerful person?
- What can we learn from Mary's response to God's invitation to 'carry' God?
- How are we called to carry God?

Friday
Waiting for the privileged to catch up

I have taken countless funerals since I was ordained nearly twenty years ago. Some of these funerals have been for the good and some for the bad; some for the relatively well known and some for the obscure. I have spotted celebrities (often trying to blend in) among the gathered mourners. Many funerals feature music – 'My Way', 'Blue Moon', 'Love of my Life' – that is off the shelf (albeit deeply important to that person or family); many use the same readings and poems; many, despite each person wanting to be remembered as unique, end up being played out in the same way as everyone else. And, you know what? That's okay. We all have a right, in this day and age, to have our funeral as we wish.

It's probably inevitable that, after participating in so many funerals, few stand out for me. But I want to talk about one that did – and for unexpected reasons. It was not a tragic funeral, such as that of a child or a teenager. It was not a funeral of someone I loved deeply and personally, like that of my dad or some of my friends. It was most definitely not a funeral of someone who was famous or who had done something remarkable or noteworthy – indeed, I had never actually met the person and I am sorry to say that I can't even remember his name.

The home of the deceased was a tiny flat in south Manchester in a block set aside for the retired. It smelled vaguely of smoke and there was a sense that the place had not been loved for a long time. On my visit, I was ushered by a young woman into a sitting room containing tired furniture, and it felt as if the seventies and eighties were reaching forward into the present day, refusing to depart. The deceased had been around 90 years old.

As I sat down, I went into my usual patter, establishing the names of the couple in front of me, making sure I understood their relationship to the deceased, and so on and so forth. They were really young. In their early twenties. The deceased's grandson wore a baseball cap, while his partner did most of the talking. We spoke about the deceased's life, though, to be honest, they didn't really know that much about him, and I ended up with little more than half a side of A4 notes. But they mentioned he liked country music and could I suggest something? I said I knew a lovely Brad Paisley and Dolly Parton duet, 'When I Get Where I'm Going', and they were pleased.

Towards the end of the meeting, I enquired if the couple had any questions, and the young man said with refreshing honesty that he'd never really been to a funeral before. He wanted to know what would happen on the day. I began to give an account of how things might unfold, from the moment the funeral cortège set out till the service at the crematorium.

Then I said, in the most unthinking way, 'I will be at the crem to greet you when the limousine arrives.' The grandson replied artlessly, 'We're getting the bus.'

It was simply a statement of fact. But I felt like such a pillock. Of course, the couple were not going to turn up at the crem as part of a cortège in a big black limousine. They had nothing. Grandad had had nothing. They were nice people trying to do the right thing, but they were not wealthy.

It may strike you that this seems a minor reason for remembering a funeral. I guess it is. Except I felt somehow convicted. Exposed. After a lengthy spell in middle-class suburbia, I had become so used to a particular set of assumptions about what a funeral would look like, that I'd not even considered that this young couple would do anything other than turn up in a frankly unnecessary limousine. A few years earlier, I would not have come to such blithe conclusions. I'd spent a good chunk of my late twenties and early thirties working in one of the poorest parts of Salford, while my curacy had been in a part of Manchester that was hardly salubrious.

Perhaps I shouldn't judge myself too harshly. It was, ultimately, a good and simple and, in its own way, beautiful funeral. The three of us said farewell in a dignified way. But looking back I am reminded that sometimes God waits for the privileged to catch up. I mean, on the day of my funeral visit, I thought I was so experienced as a priest that I could grasp the facts of grief and bereavement like a pro; I could read these young people and perceive what was going on for them. But I was behind the curve, and God was ahead. He was in the couple sitting there on that couch, waiting for me, in my complacency, to catch up.

God is always in the reality. God is among those about whom assumptions are made; those who do not seem to count; those who seem without power or position, privilege or control. He longs for us to cast off our ready-made ideas about what his Son is like; about what privilege and power God's Son should have; about what shape grace might take. Indeed, God often disconcerts us when we pride ourselves on thinking we know what he is up to in his holy work.

God waits for us to abandon our middle-class ideas about who is worthy of love and respect. He wants to lead us down to Bethlehem, with nothing more than our faith and an open, hopeful heart, to meet Christ in wonder and joy once again.

Prayer

O God who leads and loves us,
we know you wait for us
to trust in you and come to where
you already are. Lead us
down to Bethlehem,
to be broken open in wonder
in the company of your Son. Amen.

Questions

- We all have bias and prejudices and assumptions. Consider a time when yours were on display. How might God have wanted you to act differently?
- When has God revealed something fresh or new to you through other people?
- What can we do – prayerfully and intentionally – to address our bias and become more Christlike?

Saturday
What is shown in waiting

It is God's will that we see him and search for him; it is his will that we wait for him and trust him.[8]

As many of you will already know, *The Revelations of Divine Love* is an extraordinary volume, not least because it is the earliest surviving book written by a woman in English. It comprises the 'Revelations' or 'Shewings' of the medieval mystic Mother Julian of Norwich. On 8 May 1373, at the age of 30, Julian was presumed to be on her deathbed, and a priest attended to administer the last rites. As he held a crucifix above the foot of her bed, Julian started to lose her sight and feel physically numb. Gazing on the crucifix, she saw the figure of Jesus begin to bleed. Over the next several hours, Julian had a series of fifteen visions of Jesus, and a sixteenth the following night. She completely recovered from her illness on 13 May.

Though Julian's background was privileged, the revelations she received were not the product of comfortable piety. Her life was shaped through an intense experience of personal loss, as well as ill health, in a world marked by war, turmoil and plague (not unlike our own). Christendom had been turned upside down by the Black Death, and in England the Peasants' Revolt, and the suppression of the first Bible in English and those who supported it, unsettled what many presumed to be the natural order. It is perhaps unsurprising, then, that the visions Julian received were of Christ in his great suffering and Passion. Indeed, the words above from the Second Revelation were written in response to her vision of Jesus' face covered in spittle and blood, dust and bruises, with insults thrown his way. Julian tells us that it was a physical vision but clouded and dim. This troubled her as she wanted to see her Lord more clearly. However, she was told in the Revelation, that if God wanted to show her more, he would be her light. She was invited to search for him.

In an attempt to unpack this, she writes:

This vision taught me that God is very pleased when we continually search for him. We cannot do more than seek, suffer and trust and this itself is the work of the Holy Spirit in the soul. And the brilliance of finding him – that comes from the Spirit's special grace, when it is his will. Seeking with faith, hope and love pleases our Lord and finding him pleases the soul, filling it full of joy. And so I learnt that as long as God allows us to struggle on this earth, seeking is as good as seeing.[9]

'Seeking is as good as seeing.' I wonder how readily we believe that extraordinary insight of Julian's, discovered in the midst of her suffering? We are told, 'Seek and you shall find', but so often such searching can feel forlorn, in this life at least. When I was a parish priest, I supported many people who longed for peace of mind or to find some stability. Yet, though they prayed fervently, they never seemed to find – or even draw close – to what they were looking for. On a wider community level, the search for justice can feel even more futile. I remember, when I lived in Jamaica thirty years ago, just how startled I was by the stories and lived realities of friends and neighbours whose ancestors had been slaves, and whose own lives were still scarred by the impact of that history. What really shocked me was the sense of inter-generational trauma and the costly impact of justice and restitution deferred. Seeking after what is right and seeing what is right done are not the same thing. 'How long, O Lord, how long?' is the cry for justice of all marginalised peoples throughout the generations.

Nonetheless, Julian invites us to dwell in the dignity, beauty and truth of searching after God and his goodness. This is a way of seeking where – in the midst of all the seemingly important and crucial matters of this world – we centre on Jesus Christ and getting to know him better. In our quest for the Prince of Peace and the one who takes all our transgressions on him, we somehow – perhaps mysteriously and certainly mystically – draw closer to God. Julian says, 'It is God's will that we see him and search for him; it is his will that we wait for him and trust him.' From her deep encounter with God, she reminds us that God does not wish us to be separated from his love and passion. God desires us. However, in this life, even great mystics see our Lord through a veil. This experience of limit and limitation is not a reason for losing heart, however; rather it is a way marker on our path to deeper knowing. The glory and wonder of God is such that to catch a glimpse as he passes by – as Moses experienced when he hid in the cleft of the rock – is too much. Yet the woman who dared to touch the hem of Jesus' garment experienced blessing and grace. Julian inspires me to want to be a person who cries out to God, 'Let me stay close to thee, O Lord ... close enough to see and touch that single thread.'

I am so moved by Julian's words, 'it is his will that we wait for him and trust him'. I read them as tender and humble. We are not required to wait for God because he wants to keep us hanging on; he has no wish for us to be on tenterhooks. Rather, God's desire that we wait for him and trust him stems from his love for us as frail creatures, negotiating the limits of being human. So often, we are not ready for God's goodness. We are inclined to make him small in order to make sense of him, but his glory and grace break out of our limitations. Just when we think we've got God where we want him, he rises from the dead! Perhaps the greatest shock of all, though, is that the God who greets us at Christmas is not a person we can manage or control. This is no king with a resplendent entourage and acres of bling, or some powerful warlord or articulate leader. Incredibly, he comes among us as a babe in arms. The God who created and sustains the universe, miraculously and marvellously enters our world as one we can carry but cannot contain.

Prayer

O Christ our sibling,
show us your mercy and love;
when we find ourselves

in the darkness of unknowing,
help us to wait for you in trust
till you come to us
bringing comfort and good news. Amen.

Questions

- 'It is his will that we wait for him and trust him.' How do you respond to Julian's words about Jesus? Why?
- Julian found that in the midst of suffering Jesus drew close. What can that tell us about waiting, faith and God's grace?
- Julian seems to suggest that searching for God is as important as finding him. How much do you agree with that idea? Why?

The Second Sunday of Advent
The discomfort of waiting

This Advent moon shines cold and clear,
These Advent nights are long;
Our lamps have burned year after year
And still their flame is strong.
'Watchman, what of the night?' we cry,
Heart-sick with hope deferred:
'No speaking signs are in the sky,'
Is still the watchman's word.

The Porter watches at the gate,
The servants watch within;
The watch is long betimes and late,
The prize is slow to win.
'Watchman, what of the night?' But still
His answer sounds the same:
'No daybreak tops the utmost hill,
Nor pale our lamps of flame.'

One to another hear them speak
The patient virgins wise:
'Surely He is not far to seek'—
'All night we watch and rise.'
'The days are evil looking back,
The coming days are dim;
Yet count we not His promise slack,
But watch and wait for Him.'[1]

Watching and waiting for something does not necessarily have positive implications. Indeed, in medieval Anglo-Norman and Old French, *waitier* could denote watching with hostile intent. The word was closely related to *gaitier*, meaning to be on one's guard or lie in wait for. From the fourteenth century, it had implications of ambush and trap.

Notwithstanding these linguistic snares and complexities, those of us who follow Christ are called to be watchers, sentinels or watchmen. If we are pursuing the star of Christ towards Christmas and the new creation, we cannot ignore this beckoning to alertness and attention. Indeed, it is telling that one dimension of the 'character' of priesthood, rehearsed at all ordinations by the bishop, is the call to be sentinels or watchers. In the days when I helped prepare deacons for priesthood, it was the characteristic of priestly ministry most were indifferent about; the pastoral or proclamatory dimensions drew people much more than the injunction 'to watch for the signs of God's new creation'. However, I am fairly convinced that a willingness to be still, to be alert and to look out for the creativity of God in the world – perhaps precisely in those situations that are most uncomfortable and troubling – is the foundation of our pastoral call and action. Out of that attention comes both solidarity and transformation.

As we watch and wait for signs, we are caught in the in-between of the old world that is passing away and the world in which God is making all things new. One of my favourite works by Christina Rossetti is the poem quoted above, 'Advent' (1858), which demonstrates not only her mastery of poetic form but her dazzling grasp of the drama of waiting, as she holds – quite beautifully – the tension of waiting and watching for that which is here and that which is yet to come. The poem is a masterpiece of engagement and movement, enabling the reader to participate deeply and richly in the watching, waiting and wonder of the season.

'Advent' presents the drama of salvation writ large, with a cast of characters drawn from 'End Times' central-casting! Watchmen/watchers and 'patient virgins' gather in the flickering light of night-time, in anticipation of the coming of their Lord. Rossetti sets this drama on a 'cold and clear' December night that, even in these times of climate crisis, will resonate with a UK audience. Her speaker acknowledges the yearning for light during a season in which daylight is short and the night long. If, for some, this represents a wintry Eurocentric reading of Advent (and Christmas), I have some sympathy. On the occasion I celebrated Christmas Day in the tropics, I discovered that European festive rituals and ideas just didn't seem to work. Yet, it would be harsh to accuse Rossetti of excess Eurocentrism. Liturgical seasons have to be located somewhere because humans are simply the kind of creatures who are 'of' somewhere.

The final two stanzas of the poem capture being on the cusp of new life. Here in the borderlands, we anticipate physical birth, and in preparing to enter new territory – either literal or metaphorical or both! – we might hear cries that could be tears and laughter. Whatever their meaning, we finally respond with joy as our Lord – Love himself – calls us to arise and come away with him:

We weep because the night is long,
We laugh for day shall rise,
We sing a slow contented song
And knock at Paradise.
Weeping we hold Him fast, Who wept
For us, we hold Him fast;
And will not let Him go except
He bless us first or last.

Weeping we hold Him fast to-night;
We will not let Him go
Till daybreak smite our wearied sight
And summer smite the snow:
Then figs shall bud, and dove with dove
Shall coo the livelong day;
Then He shall say, Arise, My love,
My fair one, come away.

Prayer

O Holy God, grant us your comfort and love
as we wait for you in the night-time of our fears;
help us to hold on till you meet us
in the daybreak of your Son. Amen.

Questions

- How do you respond to the challenge to be 'watchers' or
  'sentinels' for God? Why do you react the way you do?
- At Advent we are called, in part, to wait in expectation
  for the second coming of Jesus. How easy do you find
  that? What are the challenges involved?

Monday
Waiting to breathe easy ...

Memory is imperfect. It is open to suggestion and to rearrangement as well as erasure and editing. Never has that been truer, in my personal experience, than with regard to my memories of the Covid-19 pandemic. This only became clear to me when, in the spring of 2023, a friend and colleague – who had been intimately involved in our diocese's response to the crisis – shared his retrospective thoughts on his work over the previous three years. His forensic account of the different phases of that extraordinary, often horrifying period reminded me of just how much I'd forgotten. He spoke not only of the various lockdowns – which I recalled only too well – but of the 'tier' system (what was that again?!) and the shifting nature of the rules which dominated and shaped all our lives. When he finished I realised that – whether due to feelings of trauma or simple lack of grip – many details for me had simply been lost.

But as I say, I do remember the endlessness of waiting for the various lockdowns and restrictions to end. These seemed to go on for ever in Manchester, not least because – as my friend kindly reminded me – we were trapped in the highest, most restrictive tier for the longest time. Indeed, there was, at one point, speculation that we were being held there because Manchester mayor Andy Burnham – the so-called 'King in the North' – was being punished for standing up to Downing Street.

An extra factor for me, both in terms of what I remember and what I've forgotten, was that I was advised to shield. The first lockdown was perhaps the strangest experience of my life. I was fortunate to have friends who dropped off food and said 'Hi', but, in effect, I was completely alone. I didn't go outside beyond my little garden or have physical contact with another human being for nearly a year. About twelve weeks into my isolation, a neighbour's cat wandered into the house, and I briefly left the Zoom meeting call I was on in order to shoo it out. When it just stood there and allowed me to stroke it, I almost burst into tears. That little cat was the first living creature I'd touched for months.

My friend's report on the pandemic response reminded me how scared we all were before the first vaccine came online. There was such a shortage of information, and we simply didn't know what to do for the best. The first time I went outside alone – beyond my garden wall – was in late summer 2020. I took my walk in the evening; though it was still light near 9 o'clock at night, I figured most people would be at home.

You might imagine I would feel released into joy and freedom. Rather, I felt gripped by near panic. I walked out past my front gate, all masked up and so very unsure. Disorientated by the space, I had all the confidence of a foal taking its first steps. I was anxious about meeting people. What if they carried the dread disease? What did I have to say to them? Would they see how scared I was and laugh at me? What did it even mean to be social and sociable now? Perhaps you think I'm being overly dramatic. However, as I walked out into that summer evening, I felt my breathing speed up and become tight. I am not prone to panic attacks, but I found myself concentrating hard on inhaling and exhaling, deeply and slowly.

It seemed to me as if I were the last person alive. There was no one else around. There were no cars. It was as if the world had been stripped clean of life – a strange and disconcerting experience, especially in the midst of a metropolis. For my world back then was not open fields and trees; it was tarmac and houses and everywhere paved.

As I began to find my footing, however, I felt as if a whole new world was becoming available. Though going outside was still desperately dangerous – this was months before there was a vaccine – I sensed in this odd, alien environment something of the living God inviting me into a greater hope and space; inviting me into a place where to breathe was the only thing required of me; inviting me, indeed, to breathe in the Spirit and let out fear; inviting me to receive the love of God that, in the midst of anxiety and fear, was always and ever present. Just for this moment, it had been worth the waiting to inhale and exhale easily. There would still be days to come when I knew I would struggle, but I had – that evening – a foretaste of God's goodness.

Famously, Wordsworth once said that 'Poetry is the spontaneous overflow of powerful feelings: it takes its origin from emotion recollected in tranquillity.'[2] I've never been quite sure of that definition, always wanting to resist the Romantic impulse. However, Wordsworth's dictum applies to a poem I wrote in response to that first evening out in the world after months of isolation. It captures something of the wonder and joy of receiving God's generosity after waiting in fear for so very long; it reveals a kind of personal 'flash-light' moment, my own experience of the people who walk in darkness seeing a great light.[3]

An evening prayer

Tonight, I shall be tell-all, tell how outside
Became mine, mine again, how glass
Of eyes misted and I learned breath,
O Physician heal thyself.

I shall tell all, of blue, of old roads
As if newly-laid, Jerusalem, blue of bluebottle,
Gleam of rain, who knew pavement
Could raise a body through shoe?

I shall be tell-all, hear! I touched
Neighbour's wall, *Love thy Neighbour*
As thyself, tip of finger tap, this is God
On first day in Eden, first things felt –

I did not know tree, mere sight, could be Jesu,
I am tell-all, like He who was raised
He sings Day we cannot dare yet see.
Tonight, I speak a hymnody. Behold, sky weeps.[4]

Prayer

O God, the Holy Breath,
breathe your life through us,

that we might know your abundance.
Grant us the space and time
to watch and wait for you
and attend to all that you wish
to reveal to us. Amen.

Questions

- If it is not too distressing, take time to reflect on your memories of the pandemic. Are you surprised by the things you have forgotten about it?
- Were there any positives at all from that time of distress and waiting?
- What helps you discern the presence of God in the midst of your day-to-day life? What gets in the way?

Tuesday
Waiting on God's song

Do you ever look back to yourself as a teenager and think, 'If only I'd known *that* then'? I do and I guess it's easy to be wise in hindsight. Nonetheless, if I were able to have half an hour with my rather troubled 15-year-old self, I would offer one piece of advice and one piece of affirmation: the advice would be to work much harder on learning modern languages; the affirmation would be, 'You will have zero regrets about how much time you give to learning the guitar.' I doubt I would have actually listened to my advice – I disliked French and German so much – but I hope I would have been encouraged about the guitar playing. At that point, I had a love–hate relationship with the instrument. Unable to penetrate the inner grammar of music and musicianship, I was close to giving up.

Though I rarely pick up my guitar these days – the ministry of an archdeacon is pretty much all-consuming – I know that making and creating music with others, or even playing my instrument solo, is something that brings me joy and delight. It widens my world and grants me a glimpse into other modes of speaking and listening. It took me years of hard practice and grind to recognise that music is a whole other way of giving and receiving. I've experienced this most especially when playing in an improvisational style, whether that's been jazz or space-rock or experimental progressive music.

It may seem counter-intuitive, but at the heart of improvisation there has to be a deep knowledge of musical form. It's really difficult to improvise well if you're not familiar with the basics of time signature, the relationships between different kind of instruments, and so on. However, what really, *really* matters is a preparedness to attend to what is going on in the music. To improvise well requires intense attention and, ultimately, a willingness to wait: to wait in trust for the moment, the best moment, the most exquisite moment, the cue or the beat to come in – and to play the note that matters, that will transform the melody or the riff.

I suspect most of you already appreciate that music is as much a matter of what is not played as of what is, whether in improvisational or non-improvisational mode. I imagine you've also grasped how the metaphor of waiting as a musician ... of knowing when to rest and when to play ... just off the on beat or just on the offbeat ... signals something about our vocations as people of faith.

I want to suggest that waiting matters particularly in praise and prayer. Our deepest, most abiding vocation is to worship the Lord. There is no greater joy and privilege. It is the first response and right of the community of faith, and we are most alive when we glorify God! What I find extraordinary about participating in worship and devotion is how, at its deepest, it is attention – the most complete attention we can give to that which matters most. Certainly, our worship can, at times, be frenetic (few of us who pray will not have prayed urgent petitions for a pressing situation faced by ourselves and others), but at its

43

richest and most fundamental it is about dwelling in God's reality.

It is here where the waiting on God has strong connections with what the serious musician knows but is actually something we can all grasp (and I believe in our deepest souls always comprehend): as we attend to the song God sings and wait to make our response, we find ourselves drawn into deeper relationship with him who is love and grace in this world and for all time. Like sensitive and skilled musicians, we wait to make our own contribution to the song. In our longing and desire, our petition and our worshipful thanksgiving and praise, we add our harmonies to God's abiding melody and harmonies; we find God amplifying good news in counterpoint to our longing. Our voices are 'conformed' to the Voice of the one who was and is and is to come. We discover that even as we recognise our seeming powerlessness, in prayer and worship we participate in the great and abiding work of the Christian community.

In Isaiah 40:31, the prophet says, 'but those who wait for the LORD shall renew their strength, they shall mount up with wings like eagles, they shall run and not be weary, they shall walk and not faint'. This has implications of waiting for the Lord to act; of permitting things to unfold in God's time. We might read these words, therefore, as gesturing towards God's definitive redemptive work in Jesus Christ: God foretells through Isaiah what will be done when Jesus is born the Messiah and King and Great High Priest. Equally, we can read Isaiah's words as encouragement to any of God's people during times of stress and strain.

I want, however, to place them in the frame of what I've said about music, prayer and worship. 'Those who wait on the LORD shall renew their strength ...' Waiting on the Lord is also about seeking to dwell ever more deeply in the Lord who is life in all its fullness; as we worship and pray, as we participate in God's most real and wonderful music and song, we grow, through the Holy Spirit, increasingly into the likeness of Christ.

Prayer

Spirit of God,
enable us to rest and rejoice
in your deep music, your sacred song.
May we dance with the prophets
to your homecoming tune. Amen.

Questions

- If you could go back, what advice would you give to your teenage self?
- How helpful is the image of music and improvisation as a picture of waiting with and on God?
- 'Those who wait on the LORD shall renew their strength ...' How accurately have Isaiah's words resonated in your life or in the life of someone you know? What can you learn from this?

Wednesday
Waiting to live?

If I said that waiting with and for a loved one to die could be a graced and godly thing, you might worry about me. 'I was waiting for X to die', might more commonly be interpreted as 'I was waiting for them to die so that … what? … I could be free of their influence? … receive my inheritance?' The story I want to tell today – of my former parishioners, Enid and Anne – is no grubby tale as might feature in a true-crime documentary; rather, it was an opportunity to encounter holiness and hope in the waiting.

When I started my first incumbency, Enid was one of my churchwardens. A widow in her eighties, she was a woman of immense wit, fierce clarity and generosity. Indeed, many of us will have had the joy of knowing an Enid: someone you imagine will go on and on for ever with almost undiminished energy. On what turned out to be her last Sunday, she'd been at church and was on as lively form as ever. The week progressed, full of the usual parish round, and I had to stay away overnight with a friend. When I got back, I did my usual reflex thing of checking the rectory answer-machine and found a message from Anne, Enid's close friend and next of kin, saying that Enid had called an ambulance that morning with some heart-related problem. There was a second message, left a few hours later, indicating that Enid had been told she needed surgery but was quite positive about it.

Feeling a little guilty that I'd been away when the crisis hit, I called Anne to get an update. She reported that Enid was now out of surgery and in recovery. Forty minutes later, my phone rang again. It was Anne. She had been told that things had taken a turn for the worse, and if she wanted to see Enid to say goodbye, she should go to the hospital immediately. I offered her a lift and we set off together.

We found Enid in the recovery room, surrounded by machinery, her breathing regulated by a ventilator and her body wrapped in an enormous aluminium-style blanket: she was obscured by technology. A young doctor explained the situation to Anne. There was nothing they could do to stop the bleeding. Enid would die, machinery or not, within the hour. The question was, did Anne prefer to allow Enid to be held together by machines, or would she prefer the medical staff to remove these? If they did, Enid would only live a few more minutes. I will never forget how Anne looked at me; looked to me. She was wrestling with shock and the responsibility of choosing between two decisions, for to say, 'No, leave her on the machines', was a decision too.

We gazed at each other without words for what felt like a long time. Anne always had a gritty pragmatic grace; on many occasions she had said to me, 'Rachel, tears are the price we pay for loving people.' And each of us, in our own way, loved Enid. I think I might have asked, 'Would Enid really wish to go to God surrounded by machines?' There was no need for more. Anne told the medic to remove the machinery, as I held her hand.

There is nothing to fear in death. At least, that's how it seemed that night, and how it's seemed to me on several occasions when I've had to face my own. When we're *in extremis*, a kind of grace can come to greet us.

I shall never forget the removal of the things that had kept Enid artificially alive.

Working silently as they switched off machines, removed the ventilator and took away the blanket, the nurses' actions seemed like a strange ritual dance. I was vividly reminded of Maundy Thursday's stripping of the altar, when the decorations in the sanctuary are taken away ahead of Good Friday. Then, from behind the power of modern medicine, a body emerged, exposed and frail. Anne and I sat down next to Enid and talked to her of our love for her and of God's cherishing. We thanked her for all we had received through her grace. Having taken away the marks of medical power, the nurses had left the altar of Enid's body. And I have never seen her more clearly or more graced as her breathing slowed. The sole machine left attached marked the rhythms of her heartbeat, that sign of life and love, of the very centre of our being. Slowly, oh so slowly, as the minutes passed, the pulse dropped: 60 … 55 … 40 … 37 … 20 … Anne and I fell silent in Enid's presence, witnesses to something beyond our understanding.

If there is a kind of waiting that is a form of witnessing, this was it. The great pastoral theologian W. H. Vanstone spoke about the 'stature of waiting'. That stature lies, in part, in not clinging on to another, but in granting them the freedom to leave. As we watched and waited, our friend was there and not there, and she looked in those final moments so beautiful and at peace. Then Anne said, 'That's Enid, I can see her now.' And she was gone, her being entrusted to the living God, in whom is our deepest, fullest life.

Waiting can be beautiful and, at least sometimes, it takes us to the heart of the holy.

Prayer

O Living God,
you long to make space for us
to dwell with you;
whether we are near or far
from our deaths, you watch and wait
with us, alert to the needs of your pilgrim people.
Amen.

Questions

- Many of us will have spent time 'waiting with' others as death draws near. If that is true for you, to what extent did you experience more of God's grace, rather than less?
- I suggest that 'there is nothing to fear in death'. Do you agree or disagree? Why?

Thursday
Waiting on the silence of God: Luke 1:57–80

I've always been a TV and film addict. I grew up with a TV blaring in the corner of the family home, morning, noon and night. Last time I checked, I had access to over three hundred channels on my satellite box. Since the pandemic, I've piled up online subscriptions like a greedy squirrel piles up nuts. I am never without access to something to watch. Often on a Sunday afternoon – after a busy morning at church – you can find me flicking through dozens of stations or scrolling endless subscription options in search of a programme or film to hold my attention. How often have I said to myself, 'There's nothing on!' Even when I do settle on a show, I'll pull out my laptop and watch it with one eye on my emails or social media feeds. And I haven't even told you about my addiction to podcasts … I have so many on the go.

Is 'distraction' the great modern sin? Perhaps that's too harsh. As our society has become increasingly aware of neurodiversity, we can now recognise that that there is a huge range of ways of processing reality and information. The need to mask our variation from the 'norm' has become less socially pressing. Nonetheless, I worry that I have become a human version of 'Dory', the comedy fish in Disney's *Finding Nemo*: attention span nil. I cannot be alone in forever being attracted to and distracted by the 'shiny, shiny'.

December only feeds my sense of distraction. I get caught up in the need to make ready for Christmas services, to sort out family visits and present buying, to get things tied up before the end of the year. There's nothing wrong with that, but do I really prepare the way God would like? At a time of great pressure, of many parties, of a sense of gathering momentum, I think God bids us to do one simple thing: to stop and breathe and be still. To take a beat each day. To wait on his silence.

Why is that so hard? Maybe it's because we're afraid of silence; maybe it's because we're sick to death of silence. I've heard many people who live on their own say, 'I can't bear all that quiet. That's why I have the radio on or make sure I'm really busy.' At times, I've certainly been able to identify with that. Maybe we find silence difficult because we've got so much on or we live in a busy house. But surely that makes stillness and silence even more important? They matter because God doesn't have a shouty, hectoring voice. Our God is a God of invitation, of kindness, who respects our free will.

In the book of Kings, we read the famous story of Elijah on the mountain, an incident described in the hymn 'Dear Lord and Father of mankind'. Elijah listens for God in the thunder and the lightning, and in the wind and the earthquake, and then finally hears God in the 'still small voice of calm'. My favourite translation of the Hebrew is 'Hearing God in the sound of pure silence'. Pure silence … If you live in a big city, as I do, you're going to struggle to find that! I expect there are a couple of places in the world … But what is available to all of us is attention; the kind of attention that entails slowing down, quietening up and waiting on the voice of pure silence.

Zechariah, the father of John the Baptist, has silence forced on him. He and Elizabeth have been unable to conceive a child, something I imagine a married priest in a patriarchal culture would have found shameful. Then in the midst of his dotage, the angel Gabriel appears and announces: 'Do not be afraid, Zechariah, for your prayer has been heard. Your wife Elizabeth will bear you a son, and you will name him John.'[5] Yet, Zechariah doubts. He does not trust in the good news. He cannot accept the gift of God.

I wonder if, in being forced to wait on God in silence, Zechariah was able to learn fresh things. I wonder if God revealed blessings to him that Zechariah would not otherwise have recognised. I like to imagine he learned from a voice with another kind of authority to the priestly voice he used almost unthinkingly. The voice of Elizabeth, as a mother-to-be, may have blessed him afresh precisely because it was not the classical voice of male power; it may have been one he'd never truly heard before because he had been so concerned with his own voice and work. And possibly Zechariah took time too to listen to the sound of his wife's changing body and the flutterings of the child growing within, and placed his hands on her miraculous swollen tummy.

Most of all, I'd like to believe Zechariah learned to trust that God waits for us in the silence and gives us our true voice. So when Zechariah finally spoke his blessing – when the child was born and Zechariah named him John – this pronouncement came from a deep understanding that God is faithful and the one from whom we are all truly born.

All of us, I suspect, have known situations where we have felt silenced. I've certainly experienced some as a woman. I've sat in business and church meetings where my voice has simply not been heard. Perhaps you know what it is to be told to 'shut up' by someone with more power than you. It's horrible. On other occasions, many of us may have felt that we have 'lost our voice'. Female friends of mine, who've held powerful roles but then taken time out to have a family, have repeatedly told me that they've experienced this: that though it is good to be a mum, others have begun to treat them as if a mother is all they are.

I pray that none of us are summarily silenced or lose our voice like Zechariah. However, there is blessing to be found in waiting on the pure silence of God. It can prompt us to clear away the clutter of distraction, to stop seeking after secondary things, so that we – as a community – can focus on God's vocation to justice and mercy and peace, and have life and life abundantly.

Prayer

O God, whose silence is speech,
whose stillness is love,
help me attend to your still small voice
this day; to let go of the noise
within me that gets in the way
of meeting you. Amen.

Questions

- Many people struggle with silence. Why is that? What is your relationship with silence?
- Have there been times where you have been unjustly silenced or lost your voice? How did your faith help you respond?
- Distraction might be a fact of modern life. What kind of practices might you develop to address and challenge distraction in your life?

Friday
The inequality of waiting

I have yet to meet a half-way interesting grown-up who is not prey to some level of vanity and self-delusion. We all have personal myths we live by. Clearly when our vanity gets out of kilter, though, it can reflect on us in unflattering ways; indeed, losing sight of who we really are can lead to deeply problematic and destructive outcomes. I've always suspected that would-be dictators, actual authoritarian leaders and those who exercise the greatest political and economic power in a society, are driven by their need to prove they are of value and significance. Vanity assails them.

Among the meanings of 'vanity' is 'self-conceit', 'emptiness' and 'foolish pride'. It does not take a huge amount of imagination to grasp how readily pride can drive a person to puff themselves up to the extent that they begin to treat others as lesser beings. At vanity's most extreme expression, we encounter individuals who are so prideful that they simply cannot bear to be challenged, and will actually destroy those who threaten them. All too often, such people seem to exercise great executive power.

In his famous study of the meanings of words and phrases, *A Lover's Discourse: Fragments*, the literary critic and theorist Roland Barthes, says this: 'To make someone wait: the constant prerogative of all power, "age-old pastime of humanity".'[6] Notoriously, Adolf Hitler made the Czech premier Emil Hacha wait for many hours while the former carved up Czechoslovakia, and when Hacha was eventually admitted to Hitler's presence, the latter humiliated him with a done deal. Yet, it is not only power-crazed dictators who exercise the power of forcing a person to wait. Such behaviour is well represented in literature as a key characteristic of petty bureaucrats the world over – just think of Kafkaesque apparatchiks, the pen pushers of Russian literature, or Anthony Powell's notorious British civil servant, Blackhead. Many of us prepare to encounter the inconvenience of delay in a milder form when we go through customs and checkpoints. To make someone wait is a basic power tactic, a way of exercising control over others.

I am only too aware that I'm tempted to use such petty power as I have when I'm feeling frustrated, or having a bad day, or someone has wound me up. To force someone else to wait can be cheaply satisfying. Traditionally, bureaucrats delight in doing so! But mean-spirited displays of power can go far beyond delaying someone's access to a meeting. It is clear from our news feeds that we live in a world where the truly wealthy and powerful typically get to act with impunity, while others have to wait for simple things. There are millions of people, 'little people', ordinary people, having to pick through the rubble of their lives – rubble imposed on them by the workings of controlling individuals and states – people who are waiting for bread while some have abundance.

When the magi turned up in Jerusalem from the East to pay homage to the Christ child, I imagine King Herod kept

them waiting for an audience. Better to wrong-foot his
visitors and hide behind his advisers and flunkeys, as these
strangers sought an answer to their disturbing question:
'Where is the child who has been born king of the Jews?
For we observed his star at its rising, and have come to pay
him homage.'[7] What does such a tactic buy him? Thinking
time; planning time; time for counsel; time to put on his
'best face' and most nonchalant 'power-broker' style to
conceal his fear, his wounded vanity (his secret thought,
'Am I not the king of the Jews?'), and his terror that his grip
on power is even more precarious than he fears.

Were the magi feeling harassed or intimidated when
they were admitted into Herod's presence? Perhaps. I
imagine it's more likely that they saw through the old
tyrant straight away and their main consideration became
how to get out of there quickly and safely. For tyrants always
incline towards the capricious, and Herod's courteous
diplomacy might be dispensed with at any moment. Yet, at
the deepest level, I sense the magi would have felt secure
in the integrity and authenticity of their mission. They
may even have been half expecting to find a fraud on the
throne. In seeing Herod, they are being further prepared
for the good news that will soon be shown forth to them,
as they discover the real deal elsewhere.

Whether or not Herod kept the magi kicking their
heels when they came to Jerusalem, ultimately he revealed
the malicious self-centredness of the hollowed-out and
secretly scared tyrant who uses others in pursuit of their
prideful and murderous plans. Herod had the power to
keep the magi, his servants and those he ruled waiting on

his whims; he epitomised that tendency Barthes calls 'the age-old pastime of humanity'. We will be well aware in our own time of this symptom of humanity's messed-up status and power-driven sinfulness.

What did the magi find as they finally arrived in Bethlehem? Matthew tells us that when they saw that the star had stopped, they were 'overwhelmed with joy'. It may make Herod sound too important to suggest the magi met the 'anti-Herod', but they are certainly drawn into the presence of one who will never use waiting as a cheap power move. The magi pay the baby Jesus homage, presenting their simple gifts – simple, at least, when compared to the abundance that greets them. Then they leave for their own country by another route, changed and exposed to new ways of being, in which a king comes into the world not to be served but to serve, and calls those who would follow him to do likewise.

Christ is the gift who invites us to respond with gladness. He is the king who finds a throne in the form of a manger. He is the one who strips himself clean of cheap majesty and reveals the abiding and beautiful generosity of abundant grace. He invites us, like the magi, to lay before him our gifts, such as they are.

Prayer

When the waiting is over and the child is born;
when the shepherds have gone back to the fields.
When the Magi have left their gifts and returned to
     distant lands,
when Mary and Joseph have fled Herod's wrath –

keep our hearts open, O God, to the call of your
Kingdom. Amen.[8]

Questions

- What is your experience of being 'forced' to wait by bureaucracy or individuals? Have you ever used this petty form of power? Is it ever acceptable behaviour?
- Imagine you were one of the magi meeting Herod. What would be your reaction to him?
- How is waiting on Jesus different from waiting to be seen by Herod?

Saturday
Waiting on a miracle

When I was little – up to about the age of puberty – I prayed three things night after night. I prayed, first, that there would be no nuclear war; second, that my dad's life-threatening asthma would get better; and … well, I'll tell you more about that third petition shortly. My prayers were often feverish, and desperate; they expressed a longing for God to intercede in areas which struck my child's mind as of pressing importance. It felt to me as if I was asking God – the God who I had read about in books, or been told about at school and church; the God who can do anything if he wants – for a miracle.

And 'miracle' struck me as precisely the correct word. In the early eighties, I was so sure that the world was about to be destroyed in a nuclear conflagration. I remember the leaflet 'Protect and Survive' coming through the letterbox, offering (frankly ridiculous) advice on how to get through a nuclear war. I remember the ominous TV ad that accompanied the leafleting and the ever-present sense that the Cold War could go hot at any moment. I was equally sure that my dad's health was on the edge and the work of physicians was not sufficient to ensure he would survive. I am still scarred by the death-rattle sound of him desperately trying to get his breath night after night in our little house. He would have been in his early forties then, but he sounded and looked so much older. I was terrified. 'Please God, make him well,' I prayed.

I have long been convinced that God answers prayer. I am also certain that miracles happen, having witnessed such myself. I am equally sure that thoughtful, restrained caution needs to be applied to how we expect miracles. More often than not, they are the work of God's time rather than ours, predicated on us waiting on God in such a way that we – slow creatures that we are – have an opportunity to catch up with the grace that is going ahead of us. We naturally want the instant miracle, the immediate answer to prayer. We want the sign and wonder, and I do not doubt that such extraordinary, world-shaking happenings are possible. More often, the God who invites us to wait works his marvels in the waiting.

Which brings me to my third childhood petition. My most fervent night-time prayer of all was that, when I woke up in the morning, God would have turned me into a girl. For when I was little, deep in my bones, I was a boy who desperately wanted to transition from male to female but was terrified that anyone would ever find out about this most particular longing. I prayed and prayed that God would make it right. I even prayed that God would make me happy to be a boy – anything to help me cope with the ever-present sense of desperation about my gender identity. But God seemed indifferent to my petitions, and when I became a proper teen, I put away such childish things as prayer. God, I decided, doesn't work magic. God, I decided, doesn't exist.

* * *

In my work as a priest, I've been told of miraculous healings, and I'm never quite sure what to say in response. I know the glorious and transformative power of Jesus, and do not doubt that in his company the dead have been raised and the wounded made whole. My experience of living in the household of God, however, is that those works of love and grace are rarely as dramatic or instantaneous as we'd like. Sometimes, healing does not obviously come, and I find it crass when someone suggests that its absence is predicated on a lack of faith. To be in the company of God is to embrace mystery.

My own experience of transition over thirty years ago – which I suspect some who are reading will find distressing and perhaps even wrong – has been one of gift. I have been surprised by joy. Yes, life has sometimes been incredibly difficult, but the fact that I am here, writing this is – for me – a sign of a miracle.

Sometimes, we simply have to wait on God. I often think about the child and teenager that I was, so deeply submerged in sadness. I want to tell my young self that it will be okay. That God *does* listen. God *does* attend to our prayers. But it may be in the waiting for the blessing that the blessing comes. John Donne famously said, 'in heaven it is always autumn, his mercies are ever in their maturity'.[9] It has taken me years to find my way to the blessings of God's autumn.

I cannot regret or apologise for my commitment to finding a path where I could transition from male to female. To see God in all that pain and struggle, however, is the work of a lifetime; it is a grace of maturity. God is ever merciful, and I don't say that in a pious, easy way. I say it as one who has been tested and seasoned.

Though the experience of gender transition is rare, human longing for miracle and healing is universal and deeply ingrained. In the face of desperate personal, family and global situations, we yearn for things to be sorted and made right. Those of us who follow Jesus have the additional desire for the world to know the peace of Christ which surpasses all understanding.

And that peace can and will be known. Not only for my 11-year-old self, but for everyone, I would like to echo the words of Isaiah:

> Therefore the LORD waits to be gracious to you;
>   therefore he will rise up to show mercy to you.
> For the LORD is a God of justice;
>   blessed are all those who wait for him.[10]

Prayer

O God of healing and miracle,
in you is found all life and renewal.
Renew my faith this day
and help me see the works
of your hands transforming your world. Amen.

Questions

- What is your own view on miracles? Why? Have your childhood prayers 'come true'?
- 'Miracles, more often than not, are the work of God's

time rather than ours.' To what extent to do you agree or disagree. Why?

- How has your prayer life changed over time? What has helped deepen it or made it more difficult?

The Third Sunday of Advent
'Using' the waiting?

I sing to use the Waiting
My Bonnet but to tie
And shut the Door unto my House
No more to do have I

Till His best step approaching
We journey to the Day
And tell each other how We sang
To Keep the Dark away.[1]

Emily Dickinson's writing can seem deceptively simple. She composed nearly two thousand poems – the vast majority short lyrics – though only ten were published in her lifetime. Indeed, since she died in Amherst, Massachusetts, in 1886 aged 55, Dickinson's biography has been raked over and reappraised repeatedly. The stories of her eccentricities, brilliance and growing sense of isolation as she felt ever more alienated from the world are legend (and perhaps grossly amplified).

Dickinson had a long-established habit of writing poems in the middle of the night, while her family slept. In those quiet hours, she found the imaginative space to delve deep into profound themes: death and immortality, hope and loss. 'I sing to use the Waiting' was written in the mid-1860s, when the American Civil War was at its height. Every aspect of daily existence was impacted, and Dickinson's life was marked by trauma and loss. Though she continued to have strong relationships with friends and family, increasingly she kept indoors. She took to wearing white.

The poem, at one level, offers a conventional scene: its spartan language dramatises the arrival of bedtime for a woman. The poet sings as she undertakes her ordinary night-time ritual – undressing and (we would expect) preparing for sleep. All she has to do is tie her sleeping bonnet. We sense the speaker's relief that she can now close the door to the house because the tasks of day are done. Things begin to turn a little stranger when another person is introduced. Who is he? Why has he come? Is he flesh and blood or a presence? Whatever the answer, the poet and this person will 'journey to the day' and share the story of how they both sang – individually? together? – through the night to keep the dark away.

What are we to make of this curious, almost fairytale-like poem when we read it in Advent? What first strikes me about it is its absence of punctuation and the unexpected capitalisations. These poetic decisions – not untypical for Dickinson (she was famous for her extensive use of long hyphens or em dashes) – raise as many questions as answers. Perhaps it is Dickinson's intention to wrong-foot her readers, for she seems uninterested in pleasing us. Indeed, many modern readers have been so thrown by the lack of punctuation that, on some online poetry sites, commas and semi-colons have been added, as if to offer us helpful guide ropes and safety rails.

I feel this misses the point. Dickinson's use of capitals and her lack of expected punctuation effectively bring out the oddness of waiting. I think that in capitalising Waiting, she is placing emphasis on the costliness of being forced to wait. To live in a time of waiting can be less than comfortable, especially if we are alone and in the (metaphorical) dark. Such seasons can adversely affect our inner life and sense of hope. Wonderfully, the speaker does a remarkable thing to 'use up' the waiting, to meet its challenge: she sings. Singing is always a reality shifter. People sing to help them praise, to resist, to hope and inspire, to express joy. Singing can change one's relationship with the world. Cervantes says, 'He who sings scares away his woes.'

Let's return briefly to my earlier question: who is the 'He' in this poem? One answer is God. God's pronouns are often capitalised. However, in Dickinson's poetry, God is not always a positive figure; he is sometimes designated as 'the man of noon' who seeks to control us. I think this 'He' remains mysterious, and what really matters is that 'He' shows that Dickinson is not left by herself to deal with the challenges of night. As she journeys through the darkness, seemingly alone, the coming of the mysterious stranger – whether He is imaginary, or a beloved remembrance of a friend or indeed the presence of God – lead to she and he becoming 'We' and they 'tell each other how We sang/ To Keep the Dark away.'

The psalmist says in Psalm 59:16, 'I will sing aloud of your steadfast love in the morning. For you have been a fortress for me and a refuge on the day of my distress.' And in Psalm 63:7, 'for you have been my help, and in the shadow of your wings I sing for joy'. I do not wish to co-opt Dickinson's poem simply for my own purposes, but her intense skill reminds me of the vocation to address 'Waiting' for the seeming oppressive reality it can be, and the call to sing in order to find joy with God and one another, as we respond powerfully to his love.

In the night-time of our fear, or when our sense of isolation seems great, we are encouraged to attend to the one who is approaching – Jesus Christ. Then, as the new Day draws near, we may perhaps be ready to receive those most famous words of Dickinson:

> 'Hope' is the thing with feathers –
> That perches in the soul –
> And sings the tune without the words –
> And never stops – at all –
>
> And sweetest – in the Gale – is heard –
> And sore must be the storm –
> That could abash the little Bird
> That kept so many warm –
>
> I've heard it in the chillest land –
> And on the strangest Sea –
> Yet – never – in Extremity,
> It asked a crumb – of me.[2]

Prayer

O God whose voice is sweetest of all,
sing with me through the long nights

when I wait for Day, for your Radiant Dawn,
in the Sun of Righteousness. Amen.

Questions

- Dickinson finds comfort in imagining a stranger coming to her as she waits in the dark. What are the things which help you cope when you cannot sleep or face long nights of worry or anxiety?
- In your experience, to what extent is the psalmist right when he says of God, 'you have been my help, and in the shadow of your wings I sing for joy'?

Monday
Waiting for blessing?

There are kinds of waiting that stretch on so long, you almost give up. I've had friends who have longed with every fibre of their being to have a child; to become parents with a much-loved partner; to be a mum or dad. At one level, I find it hard to grasp the sheer desperation that can attach to that desire. I am not a parent, and part of my pilgrimage of faith has entailed learning to accept that I'm not going to be one, much as I once wanted to be a mum. For some of the people I know, however, there has been a powerful sense of pain and frustration when – after trying and trying, sometimes for years – there has been no pregnancy. Or, perhaps even more painfully, a pregnancy (with all the sense of expectation, joy and promise that evokes) that has ended in miscarriage.

You will no doubt be aware that the Bible has much to say about waiting and deferred blessing. Some of the stories which move me the most are of those who seem to be caught up in lifetimes of waiting. I could speak about Abraham and Sarah, for example, but in this season of Advent I am repeatedly drawn back to Elizabeth, the wife of Zechariah (who we reflected on last Thursday). Zechariah had a public role as a priest with which to occupy himself, but what of Elizabeth? One imagines that her righteousness was to be shown in becoming a mother and, ideally, the mother of a son; that would confirm

Zechariah and Elizabeth's place as a couple who signal God's blessing and grace.

I have tried to imagine the emotional, psychological and spiritual cost to Elizabeth and her husband, as the months and years went by and no child was conceived. The kind words of Elizabeth's friends and neighbours and sisters would no doubt have moved on from, 'Don't worry, Elizabeth ... it will happen soon ... next month perhaps you'll fall pregnant', to a kind of pall of silence, till there was nothing more to say.

Perhaps, after a few years, the couple just stopped trying to conceive. Stopped talking about the possibility. Sought to ignore the gossips who whispered behind their backs. Over this season of non-blessing, did Elizabeth ultimately want to curse God and die? Did she meditate on those words in Proverbs 13:12, 'Hope deferred makes the heart sick'? I picture her carrying a silent shame where a child might have been; clinging on to busyness and seeking other ways to know God and demonstrate his love. And then, one day she was old, and the chance of blessing was gone. Perhaps she was at peace. Perhaps she felt cursed. Perhaps, in exhaustion, she simply failed to remember what she had been waiting for.

Scripture says that in the days of justice, sons and daughters will prophesy, old men will dream dreams and young men see visions. While I don't think it says directly that old women will conceive, Scripture shows that Hannah, the mother of the prophet Samuel, was ancient when she fell pregnant, while Sarah was so old when she was promised Isaac that she laughed. Elizabeth is in that line of blessing too – a sign perhaps, that even when we've forgotten that we're waiting in hope and patience, longing for goodness or justice or whatever, God abides and blesses.

I feel as if the blessing poured out on Elizabeth is offered to everyone who's ever felt afflicted and not good enough; who's ever had to keep a respectable face when the world's gone wrong; who's ever cursed God for letting them down. It is for people who will never conceive and need someone to call the world to account.

I don't say this in denial of the costly reality so many of my friends have faced, when what is sometimes seen as the most 'natural' thing in the world – falling pregnant – doesn't happen. I don't offer it as a 'There, there ... it's all right if you cannot conceive because Elizabeth exists to give you comfort.' There are so many ways of being a parent and few of them are predicated on actually bearing a child. Nor am I suggesting, in a pious way, that if you just wait long enough you will receive the blessing you desire, for sometimes the waiting goes on and on. Elizabeth reminds us, however, that blessing is inscribed in the waiting, even – perhaps especially – in the waiting which seems without end. We may not readily see it. We may curse the world for the failure of the blessing to materialise. Perhaps even, sometimes, we give up. But our God is the living God who yearns to reveal blessing to us.

We noted earlier that Proverbs 13:12 says, 'Hope deferred makes the heart sick.' It also says, 'a desire fulfilled is a tree of life'.

Prayer

O Tree of Life,
when the waiting for blessing
goes on and on, and we are tempted
to lose heart, come grow
your good news within us once again. Amen.

Questions

- Learning to live with disappointment and failure are part of life. What can we do to meet that reality with hope and faith?
- What can we learn from Elizabeth's story to help us address the realities of waiting in our own lives?

Tuesday
The stature of waiting

I am a sucker for love. Indeed, I am rather 'in love' with love. I have watched the classic 1995 BBC adaptation of *Pride and Prejudice* innumerable times; the same goes for the 1985 version of *A Room with a View*. That's before we consider how often I've read the source books for those films and other classics like *Jane Eyre*. I just adore it when people fall in love definitively. It makes me think the world is bigger and better than experience sometimes suggests.

However, for all my appreciation of Darcy and Lizzie, Lucy Honeychurch and George Emerson, et al., the older I've grown the more I've been moved by the love which survives, seemingly against the odds; the love that is tested by the cost of waiting, in which hope never quite departs but definitely wears a little thin. There is no better example of this in literature, for me, than the relationship between Anne Elliot and Captain Wentworth in Austen's *Persuasion*. In this great novel of deepening maturity and love deferred, Anne and Wentworth slowly, oh so slowly, find their way through their past hurts to come home to each other. For Anne, who spurned Wentworth in her youth (on the advice of her family), has never stopped loving him, though she has retreated into herself; as for Wentworth, when he returns from war and meets Anne again, we discover he is still hurt by her rejection. His heart is broken and his anger burns.

When, finally, Wentworth realises – having overheard Anne's conversation with his best friend – that Anne has been steadfast in her love, his letter to her is one of the most exquisite expressions of desire ever written. Its barely restrained passion and longing make my heart hurt. Its big concept – that of a soul being pierced – is elegantly articulated within the scope of Wentworth's abiding love for Anne. This is the letter of a person who has known affection, rejection and loss and what those mean, stretched out over nearly a decade of private pain and public success:

'I can listen no longer in silence. I must speak to you by such means as are within my reach. You pierce my soul. I am half agony, half hope. Tell me not that I am too late, that such precious feelings are gone for ever. I offer myself to you again with a heart even more your own than when you almost broke it eight years and a half ago. Dare not say that man forgets sooner than woman, that his love has an earlier death. I have loved none but you. Unjust I may have been, weak and resentful I have been, but never inconstant ... For you alone I think and plan. Have you not seen this? Can you fail to have understood my wishes? I had not waited even these ten days, could I have read your feelings, as I think you must have penetrated mine. I can hardly write. I am every instant hearing something which overpowers me. You sink your voice, but I can distinguish the tones of that voice, when they would be lost on others. Too good, too excellent creature! You do us justice, indeed. You do believe that there is

true attachment and constancy among men. Believe it
to be most fervent, most undeviating, in
'F. W.'

'I must go, uncertain of my fate; but I shall return
hither, or follow your party, as soon as possible. A
word, a look, will be enough to decide whether I enter
your father's house this evening, or never.'[3]

The long wait Wentworth and Anne experience before
they come back together is an exploration of the wonder of
otherness and the extraordinary price of true relationship.
When I think of the gift of knowing the people I've loved,
I'm aware that they have always exceeded any conception
I had of them, always remained somewhat unknown.
Loving relationship requires a sense that the other holds
mystery and agency. Love must exceed the temptation to
want control or predictability, for if it is love, it cannot be
coercive or forced. Love is adventurous and yet open to the
possibility of tragedy. I think of a long-term relationship
I had which came to an end. Except, I didn't want it to
end. I wanted my partner and I to try again. She did
not. Yet, because I cared for her deeply, I knew I had to
leave. There was no point clinging on. As W. H. Vanstone
writes so beautifully, 'Herein lies the poignancy of love,
and its potential tragedy. The activity of love contains
no assurance or certainty of completion: much may be
expended and little achieved.'[4]

Loving involves the risk of being hurt and left bereft,
as Anne and Wentworth find. I think this is part of

the freedom God gives us. It is part of the power of God-with-us as one of us. After I had come to faith, I looked back on my life up till then and understood, with amazement, that Jesus Christ had waited for me for such a long time to come to the point where I was ready to give my life to him. He had held on with such generosity for me to take hold of the gentle, exquisite offer of love – the truest deepest love which knocks even the most wonderful romantic kind into a cocked hat.

Whether we are naturally affectionate or not, I do think we are called to this radical openness and generosity in our own relationships. This radical way is the Way of Jesus. It is a way of gentleness and trust that reveals the character of God. It is passionate but not insistent. It is something we are invited to show towards ourselves as we seek to get to know God and ourselves better. Love is costly, but it is our vocation. Here, in the depths of Advent, faced as we are with the imminent arrival of Jesus Christ in our midst, how might we better prepare than to offer this generosity in our loving relationships?

Prayer

O Divine Wisdom, glory of God
all are born in your grace
and according to your love.
Come to us and remake our foolishness,
grant us discernment and judgement
as we await the arrival of your Son. Amen.

Questions

- How do you respond to the idea that love is our vocation? Why do you think you react the way you do?
- It has been said that we are mysteries to one another and to ourselves. Do you agree or disagree with this? Why?

Wednesday
Struggling to wait

There is something impressive about people who persist. I'm thinking of those who stick around, often despite lack of encouragement or, indeed, in the face of serious opposition and sometimes in defiance of genuine oppression. One such soul was Margery Kempe, the extraordinary medieval mystic, whose book was the first autobiography in English. She was a woman who took to wearing the white of the consecrated virgin when she was in middle age (after bearing eleven children). Put on trial for heresy at least twice, she had a talent for winding up senior bishops as well as ordinary folk. Her gift for weeping copiously as she meditated on her Lord – her 'ugly tears' – could repel as much as attract. Nonetheless, she persevered and persisted, and while most of the figures who mocked or were scared of her are long forgotten, *The Book of Margery Kempe* has become an acknowledged classic. Margery's longing to be close to Jesus was disconcerting and bold, and I think she would make most of us very uncomfortable if we met her today. At the same time, her passion for God was real and a reminder that mystical devotion is not simply for the cloistered.

I have often described myself as 'absurdly privileged' and I have the evidence trail to prove it. I am well educated and white in a society in which educated white people have a much better chance of 'getting ahead' than others. I hold a senior role in the established, that is, the privileged, Church of England. I have outlets for my ideas in print and broadcast media, and so on. Yet, I long ago realised that in all sorts of ways I am not privileged at all. I carry the trace of the working-class cringe which affects so many in our class-obsessed culture; I am a woman, I am disabled and I am a member of the LGBTQ+ community. I have – like so many – experienced barriers generated by bias and sometimes downright prejudice, because I don't easily fit in the kind of 'box' that would aid me on my journey through middle-class church and society. While I have no concept of just how horrible it must be when someone faces racism, I do know what it is to have to stick around and persist in an institution and a society that treats people like me as a threat and challenge to the status quo.

These considerations make me mindful of the words of the liberation theologian Paulo Freire in his famous book, *Pedagogy of the Oppressed*: 'As long as I fight, I am moved by hope; and if I fight with hope, then I can wait.'[5] This is not the place to get into the mechanics of a theological approach which says, essentially, that God has a bias towards the excluded and oppressed. What I am conscious of is this. If we have felt ourselves at times in one of those categories, the one place we might expect a celebration of the richness of God's family and the diversity of the body of Christ is the Church. Yet, the Church has often become a place of pain, trauma and exclusion. On those days when I see my friends struggling, or I am struggling, I remember Freire's insistence that struggling for justice, mercy and love is a way to be moved by hope; more than that, that in fighting unfair situations with hope we can find the wherewithal to wait. For 'waiting' ceases to be something that is done to us, and becomes something that is pregnant with promise and possibility.

It is one thing to struggle for a more generous sharing of the good and holy fruits of God; it is another to remind ourselves that *all* are invited to come around the table of grace. Jesus says in John 6:65, 'no one can come to me unless it is granted by the Father'. He also warns us about putting blocks in the way of anyone who wants to draw closer to God. It amazes me how some Christians seem to want to make it harder rather than simpler for people who are different from the norm to follow Christ. I still remember being told as a young LGBTQ+ person that I couldn't do so unless I committed to a solitary life without a same-sex partner. Why do so many of us who encounter prejudice stay? I guess we do because of Jesus.

In the Lukan nativity narrative, when the angels come to shepherds abiding in the fields and proclaim good tidings of great joy, they begin with reassurance. 'Do not be afraid!' is not whispered, but sung out from the heavens, showing forth the glory of God.[6] This is the greatest news that has been or ever will be! It is all the more intriguing, then, to consider how the message is communicated. Imagine if PR Advisers had existed in ancient Judea. I reckon they would have offered God rather different advice on how to get his amazing story out into the world. God's angels effectively lighting up the sky near Bethlehem with hosannas? Fine. Launching in front of the people with absolutely zero influence? You may well imagine ...

The truth is that the good news of Jesus Christ, both back in the day and now, is revealed to those who need it most. It is not sent to people who can exploit it for their own ends. It is not sent to the influential or the privileged. The shepherds in the fields who hear God's good news would have lived with levels of precariousness we can barely imagine. Their job was to be out with the flocks in the lonely places in all weathers, where wild animals might come and night-time could play tricks on the mind; where there is opportunity and space both to dream and to imagine terrible things. They are rightly terrified when they see the angel. Yet, the angel's words – do not be afraid – speak into more than their immediate terror.

The shepherds could be any of us. They are ordinary folk facing real-life challenges and everyday worries and fear. They are not grand leaders or influencers but, arguably, people on the margins. On cold nights in the hills of Judea, they have solidarity with one another but no other safety net. They are longing, rather like us, for some good news.

And the good news they and we receive extends far beyond the imaginings and plans of a modern PR strategy. This is no viral marketing campaign but rather an invitation to people, both ordinary and powerful, into the truth. If sending the good news to shepherds has symbolic resonance (in Jesus as the Good Shepherd), it also reminds us of the kind of God we serve: one whose first and primary call is to look after the vulnerable flock exposed to the world's dangers. God sends good news to people who long for salvation and safety. Who need to hear once again: 'Do not be afraid.'

Prayer

O Adonai, flame in the wilderness.
who delivers us from our wanderings;
turn over the unjust tables of our world,
redeem and remake the structures of prejudice
which bind us. Liberate us through your love. Amen.

Questions

- 'As long as I fight, I am moved by hope; and if I fight with hope, then I can wait.' What is your reaction to Freire's statement? Is there a situation in your life right now that might be transformed if you adopted his outlook?
- What does it tell us about God that he brings his message of good news to ordinary people like shepherds first?

Thursday
The frustration of waiting

A hot Friday afternoon in July. A day as far from Advent as it is possible to imagine. It feels as if everyone, just *everyone*, is on this motorway, and each last one of us is trying to get somewhere as quickly as possible. There's such a sense of hurry. Perhaps it's because the weekend beckons, or because most schools break up today for the summer. We want to pick up the kids, or get to the coast to start our holiday, or fit in the last appointment of the day, or simply finish our journey home.

Yet, along with the pent-up anticipation, a pent-up tiredness hangs in the petrol and diesel fumes. Frankly, this motorway has become little more than a car park.

I sit in the slow lane, though today all lanes are slow. The man in the car behind glares, as if he's willing me to move, despite the fact that the queue stretches on into the far distance. I sense it would relieve his frustration if I only wheeled forward a few feet. For him, progress is measured in movement, no matter how small. Meanwhile, in the lane to my right, the 'fast lane', the couple in the car next to me look exhausted. The woman in the passenger seat scrolls on her phone, in search of news or distraction. Every few minutes, we edge forward a few yards. It is going to be a very, very long afternoon.

I suspect there are few of us who have not been stuck in a traffic jam (and even fewer who could claim to enjoy the experience). The very phrase conjures pictures of being smooshed-up, like fruit reduced to jelly in a jar. In a traffic jam, there's little means of expressing our individualism through that symbol of freedom, the car, because our vehicle has been turned into a box on wheels, and we, its riders, are trapped in place, along with thousands of others. The frustrations of waiting are writ large in hazard warnings on the digital boards that punctuate our motorway system.

I would be lying if I pretended that I had a talent for rising above the irritation and dreadfulness of being stuck in a traffic jam. In well over thirty-five years of driving, I have developed no more skill at this than anyone else. As a child who grew up in the country, learning to drive and getting hold of my first 'banger' was a rite of passage that symbolised freedom; for one thing, it gave me the opportunity to get into the local town to see school friends. I've always accepted that enduring the occasional traffic jam is the price I pay for exercising choice, though now, as the climate crisis becomes more acute – not least due to our seeming addiction to dinosaur-juice-guzzling vehicles – queues generate more than frustration in me. As I wait with lots of cars, and we sit there consuming resources and going nowhere, I also feel scared.

When understood in the light of the looming climate crisis, it strikes me that the traffic jam is a symbol not only of being delayed, but of waiting to move into an unknown future. Waiting for news, both good and bad. Waiting without much expectation of things changing any time soon.

While I shall never become a master of traffic-jam frustration or anxiety, I have sought to develop a strategy which helps me connect with something greater than myself. I should explain that when I'm in my car, I'm usually alone, travelling between visits to people or places. So a hold-up can seem curiously isolating. My strategy to get round this, to help me imagine, at least, that I'm in solidarity with others, is (shades of Emily Dickinson!) to sing. I turn on some big tunes – show tunes, worship tunes, country hits, stone-cold classics, opera arias – and sing out loud. I sing with all my heart. I forget where I am and let go. I know this sounds ridiculous. At best it will seem like a distraction technique (it is). And maybe, crooning away in my driving seat is also a bit 'look at me'. Do I need to be seen? Do I crave attention? There have been times, in my younger years, when that was certainly the case.

But, yes, when I am waiting in frustration and anxiety for the queue to move and I long to be elsewhere, I sing. For me, doing so is a kind of prayer. A prayer – in which I unite my voice to the voices of Dolly and the Indigo Girls, of Maria Callas and Janet Baker (badly!), of Lin Manuel Miranda and countless others – and lose sight of boredom and frustration, depression and desperation, if only for a few minutes. When I join Nina Simone in 'I Shall Be Released' or Marvin Gaye in 'What's Going On', I find I am able to dwell in another time and space. I am lifted out of myself; I hear God speaking, and I find in my waiting, promise and possibility. If that isn't a kind of prayer I don't know what is.

A hot Friday afternoon in July. A horrible afternoon of waiting and frustration and growing, ambient anxiety as the gas guzzlers belch fumes out into a bright summer's day. An afternoon when the man behind glared at me for not edging forward when he wanted me to; when the passenger in the car to my right scrolled and scrolled her phone for news and distraction. An afternoon when we sweated and got tetchy and all just wanted to get to where we were going. Well, as we discovered when finally, finally, finally the jam came to an end, our bad afternoon was nothing compared to the desperate, possibly terminal one others had endured. The broken vehicles on the hard shoulder testified to that.

Did discovering the reason for our slow progress expose my singing as crass? Maybe. Nonetheless, it set my mind in a wider place, and as I gave voice that weary, poignant afternoon, I was better able to pray, both for those who were longing to get where they were going, and for those who, that day, had gone home to God.

I believe there is a music that pervades the universe. Even in the midst of our fallen, damaged world, it can be heard and what it sings is Love. This is the love that sustains us and beckons us towards goodness and grace.

When we sing as God's people, we draw closer to the one who sings the song of Love, always.

Prayer

O Stem of Jesse, tree of life and wonder,
bring forth your sweet and bitter fruit of hope.
In the shade of your mercy

is the promise of new life;
in your dying and living
is the birth of true freedom. Amen.

Questions

- What is your instinctive reaction to being stuck in traffic? What strategies might you adopt to be less stressed when that happens?
- Singing can set our minds in a wider space where God can meet us. What other kinds of behaviours and activities help you? What is it about them that enables you to connect with God?

Friday
Waiting to dance

For many people the arrival of *Strictly Come Dancing* on our TV screens in early autumn is the signal for the headlong tumble towards Christmas. I am slightly embarrassed to admit that when it first joined the schedules near the turn of the millennium, I was not particularly interested in it. I was a fan of the old *Come Dancing*, that glorious show I discovered as a child and secretly loved until it ended some time in the nineties.[7] The dancers were mesmeric and just so elegant. As for the assembled masses in the formation sequences, well, they staggered me: it was like viewing a very shiny and exceptionally camp heavenly dance! Now, having overcome my aversion to seeing celebrities testing their mettle on the *Strictly* dance floor, I'm glad to confirm that the rebooted show is one of my autumn fixtures.

I would be lying if I said I was anything more than a clumsy dancer, never having learned properly. I've shuffled my way through 'last dances' at school discos, head-banged and moshed at heavy metal gigs, become part of the loved-up masses at nightclubs, and once tried and really enjoyed line dancing. By way of watching *Strictly*, I am now familiar with various ballroom and Latin dances and some of their technical aspects. However, it is through a friend who loves and teaches country dancing that I've gained the most liberating theological insight into the beauty and power of dance. She and her husband run dances using John Playford's seventeenth-century *The English Dancing Master* as their guide. These dances gained enormous popularity in the eighteenth century and form the backbone of those we read about in the original novels (or see in adaptations) of *Pride and Prejudice* and *Northanger Abbey*. By turn lively, stately, formal and fun, they are the kind of dances which, in Jane Austen's rule-bound society, offered young middle-class people the best chance of meeting and conversing, touching and courting. The crucial thing I learned from my friend was that they require co-operation and place the individual in the hands of others. Each partner has to wait on and trust not only their consort but their fellow dancers too.

You may feel it is a little too obvious to say that dancing with a partner or partners is a co-operative matter! I still think it is worth pointing out. We live in a culture where 'doing my own thing' is often seen not only as good but as the norm. Certainly, we need people who are prepared to dare to 'dance' alone, metaphorically if not literally: such pioneers can surprise us and show us new things. However, the richest, most extraordinary dances are dependent on working with established forms and require a honed intimacy and trust.

Part of the glory of such shared enterprises is found (you will not be surprised to hear me say) in the waiting, though that may at first sound odd. When we watch *Strictly* we are more often than not impressed by the smooth elegance of the waltz, the stunning footwork of the quickstep or the drama of some of the Latin dances. In my feeble attempts at dancing, I have come to recognise how much subtle negotiation is involved between a couple: the partner being led has to trust in and wait on the lead of another; the person leading has, at an almost unconscious level, to wait for their partner to be ready for the next step. There is no point in the lead pressing on with the next section of the dance if their partner is not properly prepped; it will only make the dance a mess. Add in the music and the need to wait for a cue, and it's clear that the whole process of creating beauty – whether on the basis of counting or sheer refined judgement or instinct – is predicated on a kind of waiting.

One of my favourite carols is 'Tomorrow shall be my dancing day'. It first appeared in print in the early nineteenth century, though there has been recent speculation that it is medieval, with its 'see my play' perhaps being a reference to a medieval mystery play. It is a surprising carol in that it tells the story of Christ's birth, death and resurrection from a first-person perspective; it also figures his work of salvation as a dance of love, a trope which inspired Sydney Carter's 'Lord of the dance'. The opening verses explore Christ's nativity:

Tomorrow shall be my dancing day;
I would my true love did so chance
To see the legend of my play,
To call my true love to my dance;

Sing, oh! my love, oh! my love, my love, my love,
This have I done for my true love.

Then was I born of a virgin pure,
Of her I took fleshly substance
Thus was I knit to man's nature
To call my true love to my dance.

Sing, oh! my love, oh! my love, my love, my love,
This have I done for my true love.

In a manger laid, and wrapped I was
So very poor, this was my chance
Betwixt an ox and a silly poor ass
To call my true love to my dance.

Sing, oh! my love, oh! my love, my love, my love,
This have I done for my true love.[8]

Some theologians have suggested that the relationship
between the Trinity – Father, Son and Spirit – is a kind of
divine dance. However, I find this carol's vision of Jesus'
ministry as a dance even more potent. It brings the divine
into the human arena: Jesus, as one of us, undertakes an
activity familiar to all, and the carol suggests he is full
of anticipation for the unfolding of the dance of love, in
which he invites us – his lovers – to participate. 'Tomorrow
shall be my dancing day' vocalises Jesus' sense that he has
been waiting for his chance to come and love and serve.

But with Jesus 'in a manger laid', what can this dance
be like? In the first instance, he will be the dependent one,
relying on the lead of his partner/s who will take care of
him and ensure that he can make his way through the first

steps of the dance of life. Later (the other verses of the carol may be found online), it will be Jesus who leads us and calls to us in countless ways, as he proclaims, 'Sing, oh! my love, oh! my love, my love, my love, This have I done for my true love.' How will we respond to the one who loves us more completely than we can imagine? Well, the carol goes on to outline that we reject and crucify and punish him. We seemingly cannot bear the dance of love he offers – its intimacy, its trust, its requirement that each wait on the other. Yet still Jesus rises again and holds out his hand and says, come away with me and dance ... together we shall be reconciled to one another ... yesterday, today and tomorrow shall be our dancing day.

Prayer

O Key of David, O Peasant-King,
who breaks open the palaces
of the mighty and lifts up the poor;
unlock our imprisoned love,
bring hope in our doubt and fear;
may your faith in us
teach us to trust each other. Amen.

Questions

- Is the suggestion that Jesus' ministry on earth was a kind of dance helpful or unhelpful? Why do you react the way you do?
- Dancing requires waiting for cues and paying attention to music and your partner. As a metaphor for our lives as people of faith, how accurate is it?

Saturday
Waiting on table

There is a famous scene at the start of Quentin Tarantino's ultra-violent debut movie *Reservoir Dogs* where a group of men in black – whom we soon discover are actually gangsters about to undertake a heist – sit around a restaurant table and, as they finish their meal, throw tips on the table for their waitress. Except that one of them refuses to do so. He insists, 'I don't tip.' What ensues is an argument about the ethics and expectations around tipping waiting staff. The gangsters share, for the most part, a general consensus that being waiting staff is pretty much the lowest job in the United States. It is, one character argues, a job that almost anyone – especially women who might be juggling any number of complexities in their home lives – can take on (often with few questions asked). It is also catastrophically low paid. The guy who refuses to pay comes up with an increasingly shrill set of arguments about why he doesn't tip, pointing out that if we don't tip people who serve us at McDonalds, why should we tip those who wait on us at table? He holds out until, ultimately, the boss criminal insists that he coughs up.

Though I suspect some readers would find Tarantino's film a little outré (blood, slurs and strong language are sprayed everywhere), this opening scene is, in many ways, a tour de force. It includes several of the characteristic elements of Tarantino's controversial oeuvre: whip-smart and disconcertingly real dialogue, as well as compelling and unexpectedly interesting characters caught up in passionate conversation about something seemingly banal – in this case 'tipping policy'.

Perhaps there is another reason why I find this scene fascinating. One of my jobs when I was a teenager was waiting on tables. Was it the worst job I ever had? I'm not sure. However, it was a tough and revealing one. Working in what was, effectively, a local roadhouse where travellers wanted quick, hot and pretty basic food was not only unglamorous, it brought me into contact with plenty of human drama – laughter admittedly, as well as rancour, poor behaviour and plain old stupidity! On the busiest days, when queues would chain out of the building, I often preferred to work back of house, doing grim washing-up and cleaning tasks rather than dealing with customers. As an adult, I can now understand why so many people's tempers were frayed; most who crossed our threshold simply wanted to be fed quickly and cheaply to a basic standard. Yet, they could be tired and frustrated after long journeys negotiated in stuffy cars without air-con, trying to placate bored and exhausted children. It is unsurprising that many took their frustrations and resentments out on us staff after a very long day, especially when the food was delayed or service was a bit ropey.

To be one who waits on others is to be one who sees and overhears, while not really being seen; it is to find yourself in a position where you are valued for what you can deliver, not for who you are. TV shows like *Downton Abbey* and films like *Gosford Park* show this in stark forms:

they invite us into a world where those who are served and those who serve depend on one another, though the 'upstairs' lot typically get more comfortable beds. We see how those who serve and wait on others (at table, or in the drawing room) move quietly around rooms, hearing and witnessing their so-called 'betters' going about their lives and undertaking their plots and plans. In *Gosford Park*, one of the aristocratic guests is unconcerned when he is overheard having a confidential word with another guest: he says that the servant who overhears is 'nobody important'. As I discovered in my short stint waiting on tables, the server can be witness to the best and worst of human life ... the arguments ... the simmering resentments concealed beneath affectionate words like 'darling' ... the unrequited love ... the flame of awakening passion and the comfortable joy of old friendship renewed.

It is not, then, the great, the good or the important who in our world are expected to wait on table. That is the part of the servants. It never ceases to amaze me then that Jesus positions himself not as one who comes to be served but as one who serves. The Son of God's position is one who 'waits on'. When I think about the treatment that is often dished out (!) to waiting staff – the insults, the mockery, the bad pay and worse – the very idea that Jesus might be in solidarity with those who find themselves taking on such jobs is deeply moving. Yet Jesus wants us to regard the servant, rather than the one lording it over others, as a model of the deepest nature of God.

In *Gosford Park*, the formidable housekeeper, Mrs Croft, asks one of the junior servants what gift sets apart the good servant, perhaps even the great servant, from the average one. She supplies her own answer: 'the gift of anticipation'. Mrs Croft says she knows what the lords and ladies she serves want before they do. In anticipation, she provides what they need. If Mrs Croft is a great servant, Jesus is the ultimate one; not only does he know our deepest needs before we know them ourselves and provide for us, he offers us the ultimate feast – his very self in the sacrament of the Eucharist. He comes and dwells in the world which he made as one who serves, anticipating its most profound desires and longings: peace, mercy, grace and love. There is nothing that we can offer that will be sufficient return for the love he lavishes. He asks only that we give him our heart and pursue the servant way. As he pours out his love he is – more often than not – unseen and unheralded. He goes about his work of setting a great Table of Grace before us and we do not even recognise him. He waits for us and on us. When we turn away or seek to make the table smaller he does not give up. He waits for us to locate and insert that extra leaf, to dig out the 'emergency' trestles and chairs we bring out at Christmas! He waits patiently still.

Prayer

O Radiant Dawn, O Dazzling Star,
in whom the shadows of night
and the delights of day are one.
Comfort us in the dark,
illuminate us with your love,
bring your justice to birth. Amen.

Questions

- Being a servant and waiting on others is not always much fun. Has the Church made too much of these ideas as models for Christian life?
- Christ says that he came not to be served but to serve. What does this tell us about how to conduct our daily lives?

The Fourth Sunday of Advent
Jesus Christ is waiting

One of my favourite festive tunes is Noël Nouvelet. This traditional French carol is five hundred years old and sounds as transporting and mysterious as it did on the day it was written. While *nouvelet* has the same root as *Noël*, both stemming from the word for news and newness, one might translate the title as 'Christmas New Year'. Indeed, it has been seen as a New Year song. The words, however, speak of the news of the birth of the Christ child in Bethlehem and the announcement by angels to the shepherds in the fields, while looking forward to the visit of the three kings. It is a carol traditionally sung at home rather than in church. You may not think you know it. However, the tune is used to accompany both the English version of the carol, 'Sing we now of Christmas' and the Easter hymn, 'Now the green blade riseth', written in 1928 by John Macleod Campbell Crum.

The powerful Wild Goose song 'Jesus Christ is waiting' is set to the same music. Although not written, as far as I know, for Advent or Christmas, its words offer a potent challenge that is only amplified by the association of the haunting tune with this season of watching:

Jesus Christ is waiting, waiting in the streets;
no-one is his neighbour, all alone he eats.
Listen, Lord Jesus, I am lonely too.
Make me, friend or stranger, fit to wait on you.[1]

The hymn recalls those famous and startling words found in Matthew 25, which remind us that when Jesus returns in glory, he shall bring judgement:

'Come, you that are blessed by my Father, inherit the kingdom prepared for you from the foundation of the world; for I was hungry and you gave me food, I was thirsty and you gave me something to drink, I was a stranger and you welcomed me, I was naked and you gave me clothing, I was sick and you took care of me, I was in prison and you visited me.' Then the righteous will answer him, 'Lord, when was it that we saw you hungry and gave you food, or thirsty and gave you something to drink? And when was it that we saw you a stranger and welcomed you, or naked and gave you clothing? And when was it that we saw you sick or in prison and visited you?' And the king will answer them, 'Truly I tell you, just as you did it to one of the least of these who are members of my family, you did it to me.'[2]

Jesus Christ waits. He waits for us to see him and respond with mercy and love and practical grace. He waits for us to clothe him and give him food and drink. He waits as an outsider, an alien, a stranger. He waits in hospitals and in prisons. He waits for us to take seriously our vocation as the body of Christ and as people of faith to inhabit the law of love. But, in the song, Jesus waits, first and foremost, in the streets, without neighbour and friend, eating alone. I am always moved by how this vision of Jesus hanging around in the roads and alleyways is matched by the song's bold recognition that loneliness is something that can assail anyone. The person who sings this song is lonely and isolated too, longing for connection to the body of Christ.

Sometimes it is said there is an epidemic of loneliness in our society. I don't know if that's right, although it is fascinating to observe that for all the wonders of connection brought about by technology and the internet, a 2023 poll, conducted across 142 countries, indicated that nearly 25% of people aged over 15 felt lonely. I have certainly had to support folk who live with loneliness. When I was in parish ministry, I met and prayed with a lot of older people, sometimes recently bereaved, who would say that they could go for days without speaking to someone in a meaningful way. Church was often a lifeline for them.

Certainly, ours is a society that prioritises independence and control. Community, as I've mentioned previously, is typically seen as second to individuality. I make no judgement on that. Like many others, I know what it is to feel desperately alone. It can happen in the midst of crowds, or on occasions when it seems as if I should be having a good time and connecting with others. I have been single for a long time and sometimes that feels a burden and sometimes it doesn't. I fear most of all for the future. Will I be ever more wracked by isolation as I grow older? Might I fall, through my fear of vulnerability and my desire to remain independent, into a kind of self-fulfilling loneliness?

Comfortingly, the song goes on to tell us that the Christ who waits in the streets is also the one who calls:

'Who will join my journey? I will guide their feet.'
Listen, Lord Jesus, let my fears be few.
Walk one step before me; I will follow you.

Christ summons us not from places of safety but from places of exposure and vulnerability. He calls to us in the cry of a baby and in the agony of an innocent man on a cross. He calls to us to step out of our comfort zones and our fears and allow ourselves to be exposed to the reality of God and his Way. He calls to us to let go of our wilful separateness and find ourselves in the generous community of the body of Christ.

Prayer

O King of the World,
you call the nations
to the peace which surpasses understanding.
You who fashioned us
from dust and clay,
come and shape us into
your holy likeness. Amen.

Questions

- How do you feel and react when you read/sing 'Jesus Christ is waiting, waiting in the streets'?
- Do you think there is an epidemic of loneliness in our society? If so, what role can you or your church community play in addressing it?

Monday

Waiting in dependence ...
The joy of hospitality?

Almost certainly, you will have attended your fair share of school nativity plays. They're a wonderful opportunity to dramatise the birth of Jesus, as well as giving proud parents and grandparents the chance to coo over their little ones.

As a form they have evolved somewhat from the pretty 'straight' presentations common in my 1970s childhood, which generally featured Mary, Joseph, baby Jesus and the main roles from the biblical narratives. These days you can expect Marvel comic-book heroes, Barbie and any number of other iconic children's characters to turn up at the manger.

My favourite school nativity story – quite possibly apocryphal – is about the little boy who wants to play Joseph but is given the much smaller part of innkeeper. He's very unhappy and incredibly jealous of the lad who's landed the role of Joseph. On the night of the play, Joseph and Mary turn up on cue at the inn and knock on the door. 'Can we come in?' Joseph asks. Rather than deliver his appointed line about there being no room, the innkeeper replies, looking directly at Mary, 'You can, but he can't.'

One of the many aspects of the Christmas story is how it reveals the joy and value of hospitality. Indeed, the Bible makes hospitality, especially to outsiders, a fundamental ethical commitment of God's community. In Leviticus 19:34, God says to Moses and the people of God, 'The alien who resides with you shall be to you as the citizen among you; you shall love the alien as yourself, for you were aliens in the land of Egypt.' In the New Testament, the letter to the Hebrews famously says, 'Do not neglect to show hospitality to strangers, for by doing that some have entertained angels without knowing it.'[3] The nativity story reveals that some have entertained God-with-us unawares.

The Holy Family come to Bethlehem in great vulnerability. They have, apparently, nowhere to stay, and Jesus' makeshift cradle is a manger. Yet, there is no mention of a stable in the gospel record; no dialogue between an innkeeper and the Holy Family. Tradition has filled the gaps in the narrative with the image of an outhouse, the Holy Family surrounded by animals, emphasising their exposure and humility. It is a powerful image, though it would surely be inconceivable in Middle Eastern culture that Joseph – a son of Bethlehem – could have returned home without relatives offering his family space to lodge.

The scenes in Bethlehem model a very real and moving dependence, nonetheless. The Holy Family are in the hands of others; they wait and depend on the grace of those who grant them hospitality. The word hospitality is derived from the Latin, *hospes*, which has implications not only of host and guest but also of stranger, of one who comes seeking safety as a guest. *Hospes* is the root of words like hospice, hostel and hospital, and hospitals are by their very nature places of sanctuary. Indeed, in the Middle

Ages, they often functioned as almshouses for the needy, hostels for pilgrims, and even as schools. We see an echo of this purpose in some of the surviving foundations and almshouses in the UK.

I do not find it comfortable to be forced to wait in dependence. As someone who lives with chronic illness, I have spent more than my fair share of time in one of our great places of hospitality and sanctuary. Without the urgent and tender care of nurses, doctors and other hospital staff, I would be dead many times over; hospital has provided for me and countless others space to heal and, indeed, to be appropriately dependent and vulnerable as I wait on the grace and love of others. To be an in-patient in hospital is, by definition, to be in a place of vulnerability and dependency. There is no better or safer place for a wounded and hurting person. It was to a hostel or hospital that the man who was assaulted on the road to Jericho by bandits (in the famous parable of the good Samaritan) was taken to recover from his wounds.

In Christian terms, our places of safety, rest, healing and dependent waiting are grounded in another word derived from *hospes* – host. Jesus Christ is the host of the great feast that Christians share at Holy Communion. Indeed, one of the words used for the bread is the 'host'. Christ makes a feast of hospitality of himself, knowing from the inside that human beings need places of safety, where we can be dependent and vulnerable. In his Church, we find, or should find, the hospital for our souls, and the Blessing who will bless us when we realise that our hospitality is a response most of all to his.

I'm so glad that Jesus was born in a stable. Because my soul is so much like a stable. It is poor and in unsatisfactory condition ... Yet I believe that if Jesus can be born in a stable, maybe he can also be born in me.[4]

Prayer

O God-with-us,
bringer of joy and delight,
come dwell with us soon;
save us, renew us,
remake us according to your Love. Amen.

Questions

- 'If Jesus can be born in a stable, maybe he can also be born in me.' What do you make of Dorothy Day's statement?
- What can Jesus reveal to us about living more graciously with vulnerability and dependence?
- In what ways could you or your church practise hospitality with more effectiveness?

Tuesday: Christmas Eve
Waiting in fear and trembling

'In the beginning was the Word ...'[5]

According to many press reports, we are living through an 'epidemic of anxiety'. Some large-scale studies suggest that nearly a third of people are affected by an anxiety disorder in their lifetime, while in 2022 the Joseph Rowntree Foundation suggested that over 7 million adults in the UK had received antidepressants by 2018. I am one of those people. There was a period of about a year when I was prescribed Prozac and it really helped. Ever since, I've been aware of a predisposition towards depression.

There may be very good reasons why anxiety disorders are rife. These are precarious times, when for many people work, even well-paid work, fails to offer the means to achieve some of the basic things that previous generations assumed were part of the 'good life' – buying a house, building up savings, achieving some security for their offspring (we are told the children of today will be poorer, on average, than their parents or grandparents).

More broadly, as I've already touched on, the prospect of global environmental collapse frightens and exhausts us. We feel grief for what is yet to come, not least because the impact of climate change is already unfolding around us. We do not need to live in Brazil to be sure that each day a section of the Amazonian rainforest the size of Wales is destroyed. We do not need to be on a boat in the Pacific to know that vast fields of plastic bottles and detritus coalesce and float on the ocean. We have become so dependent on these 'organic' products that we suspect our very DNA is changing. Human beings have always been the most plastic of species; now we suspect we are being changed because we cannot expunge the micro-particles of plastic we're ingesting in food and drink and by breathing polluted air.

For the vast majority of people in a society like ours there is also this contradiction: we feel on the edge of collapse and yet we are surrounded by a magical abundance of 'stuff'. We have never possessed so much; we have never had such access to the cornucopia of creation. Most of us grew up learning the value of delayed gratification; now there's usually the option of instant supply of whatever we crave – at least at a price. However, we are haunted by the fact our need for stuff is harmful: our technologised society is eating up and heating up the earth. As I type on my doodly iPad, I am aware that my cloud storage is held in some super-cooled facility that, ironically, only adds to the warming of the planet. I want everyone to have access to the digital power I have, yet I'm aware that if they did, it would only burn through the planet's resources more rapaciously. My privilege is predicated on scarcity and exclusion. I feel paralysed. How can we escape this system of destruction? We want to be good, not least because we are well aware, via our electronic devices, of what is going on *everywhere*, all the time.

'In the beginning was the Word, and the Word was with God, and the Word was God. He was in the beginning with

God. All things came into being through him, and without him not one thing came into being.' We hear these words from the Gospel of John each Christmas. They remind us, in the midst of our fears and anxieties, that Jesus Christ was not merely a good man with a kind and gracious message; from the beginning, Christ is God's Word, who was before, is now, and shall ever be, world without end.

How does this momentous truth help us? Is it possible to dwell in the present moment of fear and anxiety and existential threat ... with hope? To wait patiently, even perhaps with joy? In essence, Jesus, as the Word of God, reminds us that our human starting point for understanding the world is not God's. We are accustomed to a chronological, 'beginning–middle–end' pattern, while God invites us to dwell in 'kairos' time. In Christian thinking, this usually means 'the appointed time in the purpose of God', when God acts.

By emptying himself into Jesus Christ, God intervenes decisively. He wonderfully reworks our understanding of reality. Through the incarnation, we are invited to participate in God's kairos rather than be overwhelmed by our human understanding of what is going on. And in Jesus' nativity and infancy, there are, of course, signs of his ultimate redemptive sacrifice for the sake of us all: he receives from the magi not only gifts which signal his kingship and priesthood, but – in the present of myrrh – his death.

God invites us to locate ourselves in the realm of Jesus Christ, whose birth, life, death and resurrection transform all things. The telling point, the pivot, is resurrection. The story of God, in which we are invited to participate, is a reminder that fear, death, anxiety – real though they are – are not the final words. We can dwell and wait in the fearsome challenges of the present because God is remaking the world in Jesus Christ. When Jesus says to let tomorrow take care of itself, he is not offering advice for those seeking serenity and mindful centring. The kingdom that is here and is yet to come is no mere rhetorical device. God's reality – in which (let me repeat) the Word was in the beginning and before the beginning, is and ever shall be, world without end – is definitive.

If this cannot be readily comprehended, if it feels overwhelming, that is as it should be. Our words are not adequate to the Word. Our metaphors, our similes, our sentences, our poetry, our novelising and word-making fall short of the language of God. As we encounter him we fall silent. God has passed by in the pillar of cloud, leaving us slack-jawed, haunted and dazed. We are undone.

This way of talking may hardly seem to address pressing matters of politics and ethics – how one might act in a world where economic and social futures seem foreclosed, whether as a result of climate crisis, or the collapse of trust in our political institutions, or the failure of economic systems. However, to be overwhelmed by the wonder of God; to confront a world coming to an end with the gift of God who is World Without End, may yet – for those with more politically and socially charged minds and bodies than mine – be a moment when poetics transforms politics.

Even if that is naive, I sense that to come before the living God as one who waits in wonder and awe represents a wiser and truer way of being than that of waiting in anxiety and impotence. As we dare to meet the Christ child – in joyous acknowledgement that he is the Word who was and is and is to come, our redeemer, priest and king – we have the opportunity to become a community of reconciliation and forgiveness. As Christmas dawns, we find ourselves renewed and transformed; readied to face and act for good in a world in need of Love's redeeming work.

Prayer

Keep us, O Lord,
while we tarry on this earth,
in a serious seeking after you,
and in an affectionate walking with you,
every day of our lives;
that when you come,
we may be found not hiding our talent,
nor serving the flesh,
nor yet asleep with our lamp unfurnished,
but waiting and longing for our Lord,
our glorious God for ever. Amen.[6]

Questions

- We are called to find our hope and promise in Jesus. How does this help us address our anxieties about the future and stir us into action?
- Insofar as there is an increasing incidence of anxiety in our society, what would genuinely help address that reality?

Christmas Day
The waiting is over

When the last present has been opened, the final sprout eaten and the promise of Christmas Day has seemingly departed in too much indulgence, or in arguments over the games table, what remains? Well, dare I say it? Everything ... For, what more could we ever want or desire than the abundance and extravagant grace of God in Jesus Christ, born to us this day?

As Dietrich Bonhoeffer reminds us,

> God is in the manger, wealth in poverty, light in darkness, succour in abandonment. No evil can befall us; whatever men may do to us, they cannot but serve the God who is secretly revealed as love and rules the world and our lives.[7]

Can we believe? Well, despite everything, and I mean everything – for Bonhoeffer himself was no stranger to the evil that people can do to one another – we are still called to believe, and yet more. Our vocation is to dwell in and live in this extraordinary disruption of the seeming ways of the world. As Bonhoeffer reminds us, in the midst of the very worst that is happening, still God is revealed as love and rules the world and our lives from the most absurd of thrones: a manger. We are called to proclaim, 'In dulci jubilo ...':

In sweet rejoicing, now sing and be glad!
Our hearts' joy lies in the manger;
And it shines like the sun in the mother's lap.
You are the Alpha and the Omega!

And how could we not? In Christ, the new light has dawned, but here is the truly wonderful thing: there is nothing to be afraid of in the night; the dark is not by its very nature bad, for God himself was knit together in the dark and warm womb where new life and promise is made. Jesus was born in the night and he illuminates all. We have waited so long for this day to dawn and now we must rejoice, even if we only glimpse the promise of God to bring his creation to fulfilment in Christ. We come back to the one who is so great that he made and sustains all creation and yet, in his grace, truth and love, he stoops low to be with us and show us all wonders in one night.

So on this joyous day, let us come back to the intimate grace Jesus offers us. Let us be like Mary, the God-bearer, who, in her love, cherished God in his dependence and need, but who also knew that she had to let him go so that he could love and serve the whole world:

Not wanting to lay him down
in the wood and cloth. Not yet.

Just one heartbeat more,
pressing the smooth skin, the pulse

of warmth she gave him,
to her breast. One last time.

before she sets him
where others may come,

squeeze his toes, touch
the curled-up possibilities of his hands.

Before he becomes
one more body.

Before the world crashes in.[8]

Prayer

God of Love,
on this glorious day,
may our waiting be at an end.
In a baby's cry and laughter
may we meet the fullness of your grace
and receive your faith,
hope and love renewed. Amen.

Notes

Introduction

1 Psalm 40:1.
2 Psalm 13:1.

The first week of Advent

1 Rachel Mann, 'Ubi caritas' from *A Kingdom of Love* (Manchester: Carcanet, 2019), p. 6.
2 Psalm 40:1.
3 Kosuke Koyama, *Three Mile an Hour God* (London: SCM Press, 2021).
4 Luke 1:28.
5 Luke 1:38.
6 For a range of views, see, for example, Marina Warner, *Alone of All Her Sex: The Myth and Cult of the Virgin Mary* (London: Vintage, 2000); Elizabeth Schüssler-Fiorenza, *In Memory of Her: A Feminist Theological Reconstruction of Christian Origins* (London: SCM Press, 1996); Nicola Slee, *The Book of Mary* (London: SPCK, 2007).
7 Luke 1:46–55.
8 Julian of Norwich, *Revelations of Divine Love*, ed. Halcyon Backhouse and Rhoda Piper (London: Hodder & Stoughton, 2009 (1987)), p. 25.
9 Julian of Norwich, *Revelations of Divine Love*, pp. 27–8.

The second week of Advent

1 Christina Rossetti, verses from 'Advent' (1858).
2 William Wordsworth, Preface, *Lyrical Ballads* (1801).
3 A reference to Isaiah 9:2.
4 Rachel Mann, *Eleanor among the Saints* (Manchester: Carcanet, 2024), p. 46.
5 Luke 1:13.
6 Roland Barthes, *A Lover's Discourse: Fragments* (London: Vintage Classics, 2002), originally published in French in 1977.
7 Matthew 2:2.
8 Originally published in Rachel Mann, *A Star-Filled Grace* (Glasgow: Wild Goose Publications, 2015).
9 John Donne, *LXXX Sermons*, 1640.
10 Isaiah 30:18.

The third week of Advent

1 Emily Dickinson, 'Waiting', *The Complete Poems* (London: Faber and Faber, 1975), p. 408.
2 Emily Dickinson, '"Hope" is the thing with feathers –', *The Complete Poems* (London: Faber and Faber, 1975), p. 116.
3 Jane Austen, *Persuasion* (London: Penguin Classics, 2011 (1998)), pp. 222–3.
4 W. H. Vanstone, *Love's Endeavour, Love's Expense* (London: Darton, Longman & Todd, 2007), p. 46.
5 Paulo Freire, *Pedagogy of the Oppressed* (London: Continuum, 1993), p. 73.
6 Luke 2:8.
7 It brought me such joy when – last year – Angela Rippon,

one of the presenters of *Come Dancing*, joined the cast of *Strictly Come Dancing*!

8 See https://hymnary.org/text/tomorrow_shall_be_my_dancing_day (accessed 08.04.24).

The fourth week of Advent

1 John L. Bell and Graham Maule, 'Jesus Christ is waiting', in *Enemy of Apathy* (Glasgow: Wild Goose Publications, 1988).

2 Matthew 25:34–40.

3 Hebrews 13:2.

4 Attributed to Catholic activist and theologian Dorothy Day.

5 John 1:1.

6 Richard Baxter (1690).

7 Dietrich Bonhoeffer, *God Is in the Manger: Reflections on Advent and Christmas* (Louisville, KY: Westminster John Knox Press, 2012).

8 Rachel Mann, 'Mary & child', *A Star-Filled Grace* (Glasgow: Wild Goose Publications, 2015).

Copyright acknowledgements

The publisher and author acknowledge with thanks permission to reproduce extracts from the following:

'An evening prayer' from Rachel Mann, *Eleanor Among the Saints* (Manchester: Carcanet, 2024). Used by permission.

'Jesus Christ is waiting' (verses 1 and 4), published in *Enemy of Apathy* (Glasgow: Wild Goose Publications, 1988), *Known Unknowns* (Glasgow: Wild Goose Publications, 2018), words: John L. Bell and Graham Maule, copyright © 1988, 2018 WGRG, Iona Community, Glasgow wildgoose.scot. Used by permission.

Prayers and 'Mary & child' from Rachel Mann, *A Star-Filled Grace* (Glasgow: Wild Goose Publications, 2015), www.ionabooks.com. Used by permission.

'Ubi caritas' from Rachel Mann, *A Kingdom of Love* (Manchester: Carcanet, 2019). Used by permission.

'Waiting' by Emily Dickinson: THE POEMS OF EMILY DICKINSON, edited by Thomas H. Johnson, Cambridge, MA: The Belknap Press of Harvard University Press,

I am grateful to the editors and publishers who have previously published small sections and excerpts included in this book:

Canterbury Press, *Church Times*, *The Christian Century*, Darton, Longman & Todd.